WORSHIP
IN
THE EARLY CHURCH

by
RALPH P. MARTIN

WILLIAM B. EERDMANS PUBLISHING COMPANY
GRAND RAPIDS

Library of Congress Cataloging in Publication Data

Martin, Ralph P.
 Worship in the early church.

 Includes index.
  1. Worship — History — Early church, ca. 30-600.
I. Title.
BV6.M37 1974   264'.01'1   75-14079
ISBN 0-8028-1613-4

Contents

Preface to Revised Edition

It is just over ten years since the first edition of this book appeared, published then by the Fleming H. Revell Company. That edition was written as an expansion of weekly articles for a British periodical. The genesis of the book explains the references in the footnotes to editions and publishers in the United Kingdom. The suggestion that the book should be republished has given an opportunity for the author to update the bibliography. While it is unfortunately not possible to revise the text (save to correct some typographical slips), the author has been pleased to mention several outstanding studies that have appeared over the last ten years or so.

The interest in Christian worship has continued over the decade; and there have been notable contributions made in the field of New Testament and Patristic scholarship as well as in the area of systematic theology (Peter Brunner's *Worship in the Name of Jesus* [Concordia, 1968] may be instanced as a full-scale treatment from the standpoint of Lutheran theology) and liturgical studies both theoretical and practical. An instance of the latter is the collection of essays, from the Catholic and Reformed traditions, in *Liturgical Renewal in the Christian Churches,* ed. M. J. Taylor (Helicon, 1967).

The nature of Christian worship has been rigorously scrutinized especially by those who deem the traditional forms (and the theology underlying traditional ways of worship) unacceptable to secular man. In particular, the concept of the numinous has been assailed, notably by J. G. Davies, *Every Day God* (S.C.M. Press, 1973), and some questions about the propriety of the term, asked in the name of philosophy of religion and the comparative study of religion, are raised by N. Smart, *The Concept of Worship* (Macmillan, 1972). On a broader front, worship and secularization have been discussed in *Studia Liturgica,* vol. 7 (1970), with an important contribution by Charles Davis.

A brief survey of *The Worship of the Early Church* by Ferdinand Hahn (Fortress Press, 1973) is rich in resource data. It contains a notable attempt to trace New Testament patterns of worship in a developmental way.

For the Old Testament background in the cult and festivals of Israel we have now the English translation of H. J. Kraus' book (see p. 11 in this book), appearing as *Worship in Israel* (John Knox Press, 1966), and mention should be made of H. H. Rowley's fine study, *Worship in Ancient Israel* (S.P.C.K., 1967).

The prayers of the early Christians have been helpfully considered by F. D. Coggan, Archbishop of Canterbury, in his *The Prayers of the New Testament* (Corpus Books, 1968). More technically, G. P. Wiles,

Paul's Intercessory Prayers (C.U.P., 1974), offers a close look at Paul's prayer language, in its form and content. The same may be said for P. T. O'Brien's forthcoming study *Pauline Thanksgivings*. There have been several important discussions of New Testament hymns since 1964. R. Deichgräber, *Gotteshymnus und Christushymnus in der frühen Christenheit* (Vandenhoeck and Ruprecht, 1967), and J. T. Sanders, *The New Testament Christological Hymns* (C.U.P., 1969), are among the leaders in this field. The study of Philippians ii, 5-11 mentioned on p. 131 has been published as number 4 in the S.N.T.S. series (1967). Representative work on specific hymnic passages in the New Testament includes: C.F.D. Moule on Philippians ii and R. H. Gundry on I Timothy iii. 16, both essays available in the Festschrift for F. F. Bruce, *Apostolic History and the Gospel* (Eerdmans, 1970), while the latest commentary on Philippians (by J.-F. Collange in the *Commentaire du Nouveau Testament* series, 1973) contains a full discussion (pp. 74-97) of the Christ-hymn, and a report on the most recent understanding of Colossians i, 15-20 may be read in my edition of the New Century Bible commentary on that epistle (Attic Press, 1974).

The standard textbook on creeds and confessions of faith in the first centuries is J. N. D. Kelly, *Early Christian Creeds*. This is now revised in a third edition (MacKay, 1972).

On baptism in early Christianity we now have the English version of R. Schnackenburg's excellent treatment *Baptism in the Thought of St. Paul* (Herder, 1964), which may be regarded, along with the re-published work of G. R. Beasley-Murray, *Baptism in the New Testament* (Eerdmans, 1972), as among the definitive modern expositions of the theme. G. Wagner's essay (referred to on p. 105) has been rendered into English as *Pauline Baptism and the Pagan Mysteries* (Oliver and Boyd, 1967). In defense of general baptism, i.e. a readiness to baptize all — especially infants — who are brought for the rite, R. R. Osborn has written in his book *Forbid Them Not* (S.P.C.K., 1967). The "baptist" view is re-stated in J. K. Howard, *New Testament Baptism* (Pickering and Inglis, 1972). J. D. G. Dunn's book *Baptism in the Holy Spirit* (Allenson, 1970) is an important treatise covering both the New Testament teaching on the Holy Spirit in relation to initiation-baptism and the gifts of the Spirit in the life and worship of the Church.

The origins of the Church's sacramental meal remain a problem for the scholarly interpreter. Issues to do with form- and redaction-criticism of the gospel narratives are prominent in recent studies, e.g. E. Schweizer's *The Lord's Supper according to the New Testament* (Fortress Press, 1967) and W. Marxsen, *The Lord's Supper as a Christological Problem* (Fortress Press, 1970). A history-of-traditions approach which is taken in the latter throws fresh light on the development of eucharistic theology and practice, but it is not free from the charge of speculation. *Eucharist and Eschatology* by G. Wainwright (Epworth Press, 1971) breaks new ground with a thorough investigation of the eschatological aspects of the Lord's Supper.

The possibility of tracing a line of development (now called a trajectory) within the New Testament period of the Church's life was first mooted by J. M. Robinson (as referred to on p. 135). His essay has now appeared in a German version in the Festschrift for E. Haenchen, *Apophoreta* (Töpelmann, 1964), under the title, "Die Hodajot-Formel in Gebet und Hymnus des Frühchristentums." The valuable essay of E. Schweizer (to which I referred on p. 135) is more easily accessible in the volume of his collected works, *Neotestamentica. German and English Essays 1951-1963* (Zwingli, 1963).

Special studies germane to the theme of early Christian worship have been provided by W. Rordorf, whose book (mentioned on p. 122) has come out in English dress as *Sunday: The History of the Day of Rest and Worship in the Earliest Centuries of the Christian Church* (Westminster Press, 1968), and for a popular treatment of Sunday see P. K. Jewett, *The Lord's Day* (Eerdmans, 1971). Studies in the celebration of Easter in the early Church are found in W. Huber, *Passa und Ostern* (Töpelmann, 1969). The series *Traditio Christiana* contains a very useful citation of biblical, subapostolic, patristic and conciliar data to do with sabbath and Sunday in *Sabbat et dimanche dans l'église ancienne,* ed. W. Rordorf (Delachaux and Niestlé, 1972).

Finally, the relevance of worship in the Church today is receiving attention. We may instance J. G. Davies, *Worship and Mission* (Association Press, 1967), J. Killinger, *Leave It to the Spirit* (Harper and Row, 1971), and J. F. White, *New Forms of Worship* (Abingdon, 1971). Three books will be of special value in gaining insights into the application of the theology of worship to pastoral concerns: J.-J. von Allmen, *Worship: Its Theology and Practice* (O.U.P., New York, 1965), S. F. Winward, *The Reformation of our Worship* (John Knox Press, 1965), and P. W. Hoon, *The Integrity of Worship* (Abingdon, 1971). The last named is particularly timely with its insistence that, amid liturgical experimentation and flux, we should not lose the essentially theological character of our worshiping activity. The heartbeat of all liturgy is felt as the Church shapes its worship in response to its understanding of God's action in Jesus Christ. "If we do not get our thinking right at the point of Christology, we are not likely to get it right anywhere" is a well-spoken sentence, which the present author would like to appropriate as his conviction too as his book is reissued.

Fuller Theological Seminary, Pasadena, California

Ralph P. Martin

Introduction

Some prominent features of the present-day religious scene confirm the impression that there is a sustained interest in the subject of Christian worship. Among these may be listed the following: the Liturgical Reform movement, originally a Roman Catholic concern at the beginning of the century but now embracing a wider, ecumenical constituency; experiments of the monastic Reformed community at Taizé; in this country and abroad, within the Anglican communion, the growth of the 'Parish Eucharist' with its objectives of restoring an ideal of Sunday worship through family participation and fostering (on the lines of the ancient Agape) of Christian fellowship among Church people; a revival of interest in a more systematic 'Order of service' among the non-liturgical Churches; the devising and introduction of new service-books which gather into a comprehensive unity many of the older traditions, e.g., the Liturgy of the Church of South India; and the issuing of journals and books (like the series *Ecumenical Studies in Worship*) devoted to the study of liturgical matters.

Important as these features are, pride of place must be given to the increasing apprehension among Christians of the nature of the Church as a worshipping community, called into being by God Himself not as a social institution or a convenient meeting-place for those whose individual interest and religious experience draw them together but as the body of Christ in the world. The Church of Jesus Christ is by definition the people of God called by Him to offer up spiritual sacrifices acceptable through Jesus Christ, and to proclaim the wonderful works of His grace (1 Peter ii, 5-9).

As a preliminary inquiry to any assessment of the contemporary interest and vogue, the following pages (which are a revised and expanded version of the Bible study course in *The Life of Faith* weekly paper) are offered as an introduction to what the New Testament teaches concerning the early Christian principles and practices of corporate worship. Little attempt is made to apply the results of our investigation to present-day needs, but it is the author's hope that this Bible study will convey its own message to the interested reader and

serve to quicken a practical concern in the life and worship of
our Churches today.

The notes appended to the text are for the convenience of
any who would like to read further in this subject, but may be
ignored if the reader so chooses. Of greater importance are the
Scriptural references which are integral to the author's purpose
in writing these chapters.

It is a pleasing duty for the author to cast up his debts and
to acknowledge the help received, in writing these pages, from
his mentors, colleagues and friends in the world of New
Testament study; the stimulus gained from discussion with
his students; and, not least, the patience of his wife and
family while the book was 'in the making'. To his wife Lily
who read the manuscript and to his elder daughter Patricia
who assisted in the compiling of the Index, the author offers
thanks and appreciation in Browning's words:

'Take them, Love, the book and me together'

R. P. M.

1

The Church – A Worshipping Community

The description of the Christian Church as 'the people of God' carries with it associations of our redemption and our destiny. We were claimed by Him, made His very own, and invested with a high dignity. Three passages from the Apostle Paul bear upon these themes:

> 'He chose us in him [the Lord Jesus Christ] before the foundation of the world, that we should be holy and blameless before him. He destined us in love to be his sons through Jesus Christ . . . we . . . have been destined and appointed to live for the praise of his glory. In him you . . . have believed . . . [and] were sealed with the promised Holy Spirit'
>
> (Ephesians i, 4 ff. R.S.V.).

> 'You are not your own; you were bought with a price. So glorify God in your body'
>
> (1 Corinthians vi. 19 f. R.S.V.).

> 'We impart a secret and hidden wisdom of God, which God decreed before the ages for our glorification'
>
> (1 Corinthians ii, 7 R.S.V.).

Expressed in a sentence or two, this means: 'No longer do we belong to ourselves; we are His chosen people.' God's people address their Lord and Maker in these words: 'It is he that made us, and we are his; we are his people' (Psalm c, 3). By the ties of eternal election, physical creation, Christ's redemption, and personal response to the Gospel call, we belong to Him. All this is contained in 1 Peter ii, 9–10.

It is only part of the story of God's saving activity, for in the quotation from 1 Peter ii we must consider, not only verses 9, 10, but the whole section of the Apostle's Letter.

The Church, he shows, is a spiritual temple, erected to God's glory, and for His worship (verse 5). The Church is a holy priesthood, to offer spiritual sacrifices acceptable to God through Jesus Christ (verse 5). The Church, as partner with ancient Israel within the one covenant of grace, exists at the calling of God Himself, 'to proclaim the triumphs of him who has called you out of darkness into his marvellous light' (verse 9, N.E.B.). In fine, the Church of Christ is summoned into being by God in order to be *a worshipping community.* This fact sets the stage for our studies.

Defining The Term 'Worship'

Worship is a noble word. The term comes into our modern speech from the Anglo-Saxon *weorthscipe.* This later developed into *worthship,* and then into *worship.* It means, 'to attribute worth' to an object. We use the word loosely when we say of a man, 'He worships his money', or his car, or his golf clubs. A deeper meaning is found in the honorific title, 'His Worship the Mayor', by which we dignify the first citizen of our town or city as a person who deserves special esteem and respect. In the Marriage Service of the Book of Common Prayer, the prospective husband's promise is 'With my body I thee worship' – a pledge of utter loyalty and devotion to his bride, who is worthy of this, in his eyes. If we may elevate this thought to the realm of divine–human relationships, we have a working definition of the term worship ready-made for us. *To worship God is to ascribe to Him supreme worth,* for He alone is worthy.

The Psalms of the Old Testament re-echo this truth in many ways. 'Give unto the Lord the glory due unto His name' (Psalm xcvi, 8). Because the Lord is great, He is 'greatly to be praised' (Psalm xcvi, 4). 'Exalt the Lord our God, and worship at His holy hill' is the call of Psalm xcix, 9, with the reason supplied for this invitation to worship, 'for the Lord our God is holy'.

It is the excellent worthiness of God, therefore, which makes our worship possible; and when we offer Him our devotion, praise and prayer, this is to be the thought which is uppermost in our minds: He alone is worship-ful. We ascribe to Him all that is in keeping with His nature and revealed person. Before His august presence and His great name (Malachi i, 11), who can refuse to bow down and acknowledge that He is God alone? (1 Kings xviii, 29). The claim is laid upon all men, therefore (1 Timothy ii, 8) as God's creatures, and upon all classes of men, both young men, and maidens; old men, and children . . . Let them praise the name of the Lord: for His name alone is excellent; His glory is above the earth and heaven' (Psalm cxlviii, 12, 13).

Some Principles of Christian Worship

As we shall later have occasion to notice, the matrix of early Christian worship was the ancestral cultus and devotions of the Jewish faith, as these were seen to have been fulfilled in the coming of the Messiah. It is necessary, then, to begin with the Old Testament, the common Scriptures of both Judaism and the nascent Church.

It is not our purpose, however, to describe in detail the rites and ceremonies of the Old Testament worshipping community. For information on these matters, the books of A. S. Herbert and H. J. Kraus may be consulted.* Nor is our task to investigate the rich vocabulary which the Old Testament uses to depict the nation's worship, except to draw attention to the two prominent terms which throw light on the underlying principles of the worship.

First, the Old Testament word *hishaḥawāh* means literally 'a bowing down'; and emphasizes the way in which an Israelite fittingly thought of his approach to the holy presence of God. He bows himself down in lowly reverence and prostration. The term indeed is used of men's homage to their fellows who, as V.I.P.s, command respect (Genesis xxvii, 29; 1 Samuel xxv, 23; 2 Samuel xiv, 33; xxiv, 20); but the full significance is seen in the use of the word when it means the Hebrew's approach to God, the great King and sovereign Lord (Genesis xxiv, 52; 2 Chronicles vii, 3; xxix, 29). The Greek term, used in the Septuagint to translate *shāḥāh*, is *proskunein*, with the same overtone of submissive lowliness and deep respect.

The second term is *'abodāh*, translated 'service'. It is from the same root that the term 'slave', 'servant' (*'ebed*) is taken; and this is important. For the highest designation of the Hebrew in his engagement with the worship of God is just

* A. S. Herbert, *Worship in Ancient Israel* (Ecumenical Studies in Worship) (London, 1959); H. J. Kraus, *Gottesdienst in Israel* (Munich 1954). As the sub-title of the latter book implies, it is concerned with the meaning of the Feast of Tabernacles in Judaism.

this word 'servant'. He delighted to call himself God's *'ebed* (e.g., Psalm cxvi, 16); and expressed that joy in his acts of private and corporate praise and prayer. Unlike the Greek thought of slavery as servile abasement and captivity, the Hebrew notion, implicit in the word *'ebed*, expressed the relationship of servant and kindly master (e.g., Exodus xxi, 1–6). This bond was thought of and described in terms of privilege and honour more than of inhuman bondage; and when men called themselves the 'servants of God' in the cultic sense, they were paying tribute to the intimate and honoured relationship into which God had brought them. Thus, Israel's great leaders are so called, 'the servants of God' (especially David, Psalm lxxxix, 3, 20). The corresponding Greek term is *latreia* ('service'); and in the light of the background in the Old Testament, we should understand Paul's use of the same Greek word in Romans i, 9; xii, 1; and xv, 16, as well as his reference to Israel's worship in Romans ix, 4. He sees it as his and the Church's solemn privilege and honour to be entrusted with the service of the Gospel. That service is his offering to God of that worth and honour by which He is glorified in the salvation of the Gentiles.

From these two Bible terms we learn something of the worshipper's attitude to the command which God addresses to him. He is summoned into the presence of the Holy One of Israel; and he responds to this call with an appropriate sense of reverence, yet also with an awareness that to behold the face of God and commune with Him is an inestimable blessing and delight. Such an approach to public worship has given us the spiritual masterpieces of Psalms xlii, xliii, lxv, lxxxiv and cxxii. All these psalms strike the note of thankful acknowledgement of God and the Psalmist's joy at coming into His sanctuary.

We can probe a little deeper and discover certain fundamental principles which underlie and undergird the Biblical doctrine of worship.

I. *God Is: His Revealed Character*

The Bible's teaching on this subject begins where all Biblical teaching arises: with the doctrine of God Himself. Certain scholars have emphasized this point. J. Alan Kay observes:[*] 'Worship is man's response to the nature and action of God,' while C. E. B. Cranfield in a valuable article on the theological significance of Christian worship stresses the fact that 'through-

---

[*] J. A. Kay, *The Nature of Christian Worship* (London 1953), p. 7

out the Bible it is assumed that the initiative in true worship is God's'.* From Exodus xxix, 38–46 it seems very clear that it is God who takes the first step in proposing the way in which He is to be approached and it is His promised presence to an obedient people which ensures the communion. Worship which is man-devised and conducted according to human dictates and whims, however impressive and aesthetic it may appear, is not acceptable. The verdict upon Jeroboam's rival sanctuary at Bethel is a case in point (1 Kings xii, 33). Worshipping by the Spirit of God entails a rejecting of all 'confidence in the flesh' (Philippians iii, 3). Our first inquiry must be one which seeks to understand the character of the God whom we worship. The nature of God as He has graciously disclosed it in the pages of the Bible will determine all subsequent consideration of this subject, and will affect every phase of our desired communion with Him. Some of the main facets of God's self-revelation may be listed.

(a) He is *the living God* (e.g., Jeremiah x, 10; 1 Timothy vi, 17) – a truth more often assumed in the Scripture than explicitly stated. The entire framework and substance of God's self-disclosure rests upon this base: that He is the living God in whom all creation lives and from whom all His creatures draw their moment-by-moment existence (Daniel v, 23; Acts xvii, 25–28). Only on the basis of this fundamental postulate of the 'livingness' and reality of God may we contemplate our coming to Him in worship at all, for the statement of Hebrews xi, 6: 'He that cometh to God must believe that He is' provides the logic which all must concede. As A. M. Fairbairn put it, 'the man who does not believe that God can speak to him will not speak to God'. The fool who says in his heart that there is no God (Psalm xiv, 1; liii, 1; Job ii, 10) will never become a worshipper. How could he? The corollary of Luther's well-known dictum, 'To believe in God is to worship God', is also true. Worship is possible only on the ground of the faith that God exists.

(b) He is *majestic in His holiness.* The awe-ful holiness of God is a thread of teaching which runs through the entire Bible. In that awe-inspiring presence His servants are conscious of their finitude and frailty. Abraham confesses that he is dust and ashes (Genesis xviii, 27). Moreover, human sinfulness and shame are exposed in the light of His pure presence (Job xlii,

* C. E. B. Cranfield, art. 'Divine and Human Action. The Biblical Concept of Worship', *Interpretation*, xxii, 1958, pp. 387–98.

5, 6; Ezra ix, 5–15; Daniel ix, 3–20; Luke v, 8; Acts ix, 3, 4; Revelation i, 17); and men become conscious of their unfitness to approach the holy God in His 'numinous' power, as Rudolf Otto has designated this distinctiveness of God (see Isaiah vi, 5 for this awareness of dread and awe; compare 1 Samuel vi, 20; Jeremiah xxx, 21). Not every part of Otto's presentation of the *Idea of the Holy** is acceptable, but we may agree that there are, in the Scriptural witness, the two aspects of God's revelation which he labelled *tremendum*, i.e. the aweful manifestation of God as the Wholly Other; and *fascinans*, i.e. attracting as well as repelling. It is the first element which impresses upon us the holy 'apartness' of God, His greatness and His glory, His might and His majesty, so that we bow down before His presence and humble ourselves as those recognize that there is an immeasurable distance between ourselves as mere men whose breath is in their nostrils (Isaiah ii, 22) and Him, the Eternal and Unique God. Our approach, then, will be in the constant awareness of our weakness and sinfulness; and we shall draw near with becoming reverence and fear, as Hebrews xii, 28, 29 directs us. One cannot be 'pally', or flippant with the God who is an all-consuming fire!

(c) Yet, in the paradox of Otto's description, *the All-holy is the All-gracious*; and His love is so outstretched to us that we may come with confidence and with an answering love. Luther's agonizing quest : 'How can I secure a gracious God?' is fulfilled in the revelation of God in His Son. He is the God of all grace (1 Peter v, 10). Because of this revealed truth, we are emboldened to draw near. This is the master-theme of Hebrews, which rings out the exhortation: 'Let us come . . . draw near . . . approach unto God through our high Priest, Jesus the Son of God.' Much is made in the New Testament of the importance of Christ's advocacy and presence in heaven on His people's behalf. The Christian's access to God is thus assured (Ephesians ii, 18; Romans v, 2; 1 Peter iii, 18; Hebrews vii, 25; x, 19–22) and his prayers are offered in the name of the Son (John xv, 16; Ephesians v, 20) as well as his praises (Hebrews xiii, 15; 1 Peter ii, 6). C. E. B. Cranfield comments: 'The efficacy of our worship as our action lies in his action on our behalf, his continual intercession' (Romans viii, 34;

---

* R. Otto, *The Idea of the Holy* (Pelican Book, 1960). A recent book, *The Concept of Holiness* by O. R. Jones (London, 1961) has some pertinent criticisms of Otto's thesis.

Hebrews vii, 25; 1 John ii, 1 f.);* and the intercessory office
of Christ takes on its full meaning from the fact that He is the
Father's Son and Revelation. The One whom we worship has
made known His character in Jesus Christ through whom we
come to God.

We come therefore with confidence, not in fear, as though we
were uncertain of God. Following the older theologians, we
may put it like this. Our fellowship with God in worship is not
in servile fear, but in filial fear which leads to a holy boldness
and adoring love, but which never forgets who God is and
what we are in His sight.

(*d*) *God is unique* – and is to be worshipped to the exclusion
of all else. This is the meaning of the term 'jealousy' when
applied to Him in the rubric of Exodus xx, 5. See too Isaiah
xlii, 8. The New Testament carries forward this theme of God's
unique glory, which makes idolatry a crime of *lese-majesty*,
and His sole right to be praised by all living creatures (Revelation iv, 10, 11; v, 13). Paul's stringent warning to the Corinthian
believers who found no difficulty in sharing a meal in an idol-
temple and eating food consecrated to the heathen god is
clear: 'Flee from idolatry' (1 Corinthians x, 14). There is an
exclusiveness about loyalty to Christ which must be honoured
at all costs (1 Corinthians x, 21). If this reverence for the Lord
is exclusive, and the worship rendered to Him is total, then it
follows that men must not be unduly honoured (Acts x, 25,
26; xiv, 11–18; 1 Corinthians iii, 5, 21); nor angels accorded a
dignity which usurps the place of God (Colossians ii, 18;
Revelation xxii, 9; Hebrews i, 1–14).

The New Testament writers know that there are those who
defiantly put themselves in the place of God and seek to claim
the homage and service of men (Acts xii, 21–23). The chiefest
of these is Satan (Matthew iv, 9) who tries to divert our devotion away from God to himself. But the choice is clear-cut:
'You cannot serve God and mammon' (Matthew vi, 24). However 2 Thessalonians ii, 1–12 is to be taken, whether 'the man
of lawlessness' was present in Paul's day, or is yet to appear,
the senseless aspiration of one who claims to be God is somewhat parallel with the status of the beast of the Apocalypse
who is worshipped and whose mouth is filled with blasphemies
(Revelation xiii, 4 ff.). And in both cases their end is sure
(2 Thessalonians ii, 8, 9; Revelation xx, 10).

True worship, then, is offered in the New Testament Church

* C. E. B. Cranfield, article quoted, p. 391

to 'the King of ages, immortal, invisible, the only God' (1 Timothy i, 17). Yet the invisible God has disclosed His nature in His Son (John i, 18; 2 Corinthians iv. 4–6; Colossians i, 15). In Christ we have the perfect picture of God in human form, so that our worship is related to One whose character is appreciable and real; and through Christ we are enabled to come to God. This opens before us naturally the subject of God's redeeming acts.

II. *God Gives: His Gracious Gifts*

We turn now to face the question, Why should we worship God? from a new angle. We desire to offer Him our thanksgiving because He has bestowed His gifts so signally upon us. Worship is the response we make to the gifts of God. The Bible's teaching is embarrassingly rich. God daily loadeth us with His benefits, sings the Psalmist (Psalm lxviii, 19); and in our worship we acknowledge that He is the Giver of every good and perfect gift (James i, 17). He does good, giving us rain from heaven and fruitful seasons (Acts xiv, 17). Much of the Old Testament is taken up with this theme of God's care in the provision of human needs; and the so-called 'Nature Psalms' are tributes to God's providence (e.g., Psalm civ, especially verses 14 ff.). Yet God is praised, even in the context of His material provision, for the blessings of the covenant. Deuteronomy xxvi, 1 ff. is of special value here, as it shows how, embedded in the rite of the offering of the first-fruits, is a credal confession (verses 5–9) which celebrates the election, calling and redemption of Israel and the installation of the nation in the land of divine promise.

The New Testament books highlight the spiritual enrichments of life. The exultant outbursts of Ephesians i, 3 ff. and 1 Peter i, 3 ff. centre our thoughts upon God's saving mercy in Christ and the Gospel. The bounty of God's care and provision is indeed recorded, especially in the teaching of Jesus (e.g., Luke xii, 22–31); and the God's creative and sustaining power in nature is a theme of the heavenly anthem (Revelation iv, 11), but there can be no doubt as to the centre of gravity in New Testament teaching on worship. The lodestone which irresistibly draws the New Testament Church to the recognition of God's love and mercy is His saving action in the Son of His love. Luther's limpid confession of faith, 'Christ the Son of God is our Saviour' is sufficient to call forth the loudest and most triumphant chords of worship and praise. Christian worship finds here its true centre and its main inspiration,* as it celebrates that mighty act of redemption in Christ – incarnate, atoning and exalted (these are the motifs of the 'new song' of the redeemed in Revelation v, 9–14); and His continuing presence with His people in the Holy Spirit makes our worship a reality and not (as it would otherwise be) an empty form (Philippians iii, 3).

III. *God Expects: His Imperious Claim*

Because of what God has done for us – He has loved us, saved us, blessed us, kept us – and is still doing, we owe it to Him to offer our tributes of corporate praise and prayer. As the Apostle reasons in Romans xii, 1, because we have known the mercies of God (set forth in the preceding chapters of Romans), we are called upon to yield our lives as a living sacrifice. This is our spiritual worship (as the R.S.V. renders). At this point duty and privilege meet and coalesce. We owe our worship to God for He alone deserves to be praised 'from the rising of the sun to the going down of the same' (Malachi i, 11). But this claim which He lays upon is is no irksome task and uncongenial duty which we accept with reluctance and distaste. Rather, it is our supreme delight and joyous office to respond to His claim upon us as His people. So far from murmuring and complaining as the Jewish people did (as in Psalm l, and Micah vi) when the ritual made demands upon them, let us follow the better example of those who were glad when the call was issued, 'Let us go up unto the house of the Lord' (Psalm cxxii); and who found it to be their greatest pleasure to mingle in the courts of the holy place (Psalm lxxxiv).

Christian worship, then, is the happy blend of offering to God our Creator and Redeemer through Jesus Christ both what we owe to Him and what we would desire to give Him.

> No gift have we to offer
> For all Thy love imparts,
> But that which Thou desirest,
> Our humble, thankful hearts.

* C. E. B. Cranfield's reminder is timely, therefore: 'One of the worst forms of ingratitude is to be so occupied with thanking God for his innumerable lesser mercies that we have little time left for thanking him for his supreme Gift,' article quoted, p. 394.

2

The Jewish Inheritance in the Temple and Synagogue

The first Christian society at Jerusalem began its existence as a group within the framework of the ancestral Jewish faith. At least, so it seemed to all outward appearance, for Tertullus, the hired 'devil's advocate', refers derisively to Paul as 'a ringleader of the sect of the Nazarenes' (Acts xxiv, 5); and later verses in the Acts of the Apostles confirm that, in the eyes of the Jews, the earliest Christian Church looked like a party within the Jewish fold. The same word, translated as 'sect' in Acts xxiv, 5 and xxviii, 22 and as 'heresy' in xxiv, 14, is the regular term for a party within Judaism. Thus in Acts v, 17 we read of the party of the Sadducees and in xv, 5 and xxvi, 5 of the party of the Pharisees (see, too, Josephus, *Ant.* xviii. 1 for these groups along with the Essenes and 'fourth philosophy' = the Zealots). There was nothing, on the face of it, which would strike strange about the congregating of like-minded Jews as a band of Nazarenes.

Yet there was one distinguishing feature which marked out these people from other Jewish 'sects'. This was their adherence to the belief that the Messiah had come, and that His name was Jesus of Nazareth. Hence the title 'Nazarene' seems best explained by their devotion to Him as the Messiah who hailed from Nazareth (Acts ii, 22; cf. Matthew ii, 23). Yet, in the early days of the Church's life, there seems to have been no desire to leave the parent religion – at least as far as the outward practice of the faith was concerned. The followers of the risen Lord 'continued steadfastly in prayer' (Acts i, 14), a verse which implies that the first believers were diligent at the 'prayer-assembly'. The Greek term used here is a regular one for the Jewish synagogue fellowship (Acts xvi, 13, 16); and some scholars have drawn the inference from this word that the disciples in Jerusalem formed themselves into a synagogue.* The Mishnah law makes it possible for ten male Jews anywhere to form a synagogue, and there was nothing schismatic about this action. The description given in Acts ii, 42–47 suggests a continuance in the Temple services (compare Luke xxiv, 52, 53; Acts iii, 1), and the use of the Temple adjuncts to worship, along with such distinctively Christian practices as 'the breaking of bread' (Acts ii, 42, 46) and prayers in the name of Jesus (Acts iv, 24–30).

As the Church grew and enlarged its borders in the formation, under God, of Christian communities outside Jerusalem, it received into its fellowship those whose religious and cultural background was shaped by the synagogue. The earliest converts outside the holy city were evidently drawn from sections of Jewish life most influenced by the synagogue worship. These were the Jewish proselytes, i.e. Gentiles who expressed a desire to become Jews by the procedure of an obedience to the Law, circumcision and a ritual baptism; and, as a separate class, the 'God-fearers' (as they are termed in Acts x, 22; xiii, 16), i.e. those on the fringe of the Jewish religion, attracted to it and sympathetic with it, but not sufficiently convinced to take the decisive steps of a full committal. For these men and women who were familiar with the traditions of the Jewish faith and cultus in the synagogue, no less than for those who attended the Temple services in the capital city (see Acts vi, 7 for the accession to the Church of 'a great company of the priests'), there would be no need to invent new forms of worship. Christianity entered into the inheritance of an already existing pattern of worship, provided by the Temple ritual and synagogue Liturgy, even as it built upon the fundamental Judaic tenets which so impressed the converts to that faith, namely belief in one, righteous God and His call to His people that their lives should be holy and pure. T. W. Manson's conclusion may be quoted: 'The first disciples were Jews by birth and upbringing, and it is *a priori* probable that they would bring into the new community some at least of the religious usages to which they had long been accustomed.'† The background of early Christian worship must be sought in these two Jewish institutions of the Temple and the synagogue.

* Lake and Jackson, *The Beginnings of Christianity*, Vol. I (London, 1920), p. 304.

† T. W. Manson, art. 'The Jewish Background', *Christian Worship*: *Studies in its History and Meaning*, ed. N. Micklem (Oxford, 1936), p. 35.

I. *The Place of the Temple*

It is a singular fact that the New Testament writers maintain an attitude of distinct reserve to the Temple cult. In the mission and ministry of Jesus, He was concerned about the sanctity of the Temple of God. He called it, 'My Father's house' (Luke ii, 49, R.V.); and the same sense of reverence for the building as the habitation of Israel's God is expressed by the disciple's remark in Mark xiii, 1: 'Look, Teacher, what wonderful stones and what wonderful buildings! The Rabbis exclaim with a pardonable exaggeration: 'He who has not seen the Holy Place in its full construction has never seen a splendid building in his life!'[*] for Josephus pays tribute to the way in which visitors to the capital city were immediately impressed by the architecture of the Temple and its precincts.[†] Our Lord worshipped there at the appointed festivals and holy days (John ii, 13 ff.; vii, 2 ff.; x, 22 and, of course, there is the record of His final entry into the city and the last Passover meal). He clearly attached great importance to its central place in the spiritual life of His own race whose ancient traditions He valued (cf. John iv, 22; Romans ix, 4, 5; Galatians iv, 4).

Yet there is no indisputable evidence that He ever offered sacrifice in the Temple, and much evidence to show that He broke, at some decisive points, with the Rabbinical orthodoxy of the Jerusalem Temple authorities. The test-case is the observance of the final meal with His disciples which, while it had many features of a Passover feast, was not apparently the regular Paschal celebration. We shall be concerned with this matter when we come to the Lord's Supper in the early Church, which is connected with the Lord's last Supper. It will be enough now to draw attention to one surprising feature and omission from the last meal in the Upper Room. Although the disciples are bidden to 'prepare the passover' (Mark xiv, 12; Luke xxii, 7) in the Upper Room, the subsequent meal is described with no allusion to a lamb. Yet the Rabbinical regulation prescribes that three things are necessary for the Passover: a lamb which must have been ritually slaughtered in the Temple precincts, unleavened bread, and bitter herbs. How is the omission of the first element to be explained,

---

[*] *b. Sukkah* 51 b. cited by W. Grundmann, *Das Evangelium nach Markus* (Berlin, 1962), p. 262.

[†] See *The Jewish War*, Bk. V, Chap. 5, especially sect. 6.

for the other parts of the service are explicitly referred to?

Two recent scholars have offered the following explanations. E. Stauffer* has drawn attention to the Jewish law which forbade an apostate to partake of the Paschal lamb, although this same law allowed him to eat unleavened bread and bitter herbs. In the eyes of the Rabbis, Jesus was such an apostate and would have been precluded from obtaining a lamb from the Temple authorities. Stauffer also notices that the possibilities of a celebration of Passover without a lamb are mentioned in first century literature; and this point has been taken up by B. Gärtner in his study of John vi.† Josephus, for instance, considers the possibility of a Passover meal outside Jerusalem, in the Dispersion of the Jews, where a ritually slaughtered lamb would not be available; and it is even suggested that, without a lamb, a valid Passover may be observed. Our Lord's background as a Galilean Jew would endorse the supposition that He did not conform rigidly to the Jerusalem pattern of celebration; and this is confirmed by His Passover meals in Galilee (e.g., in John vi). Whilst, therefore, He revered the Temple as His Father's house, it held for Him no indispensable place and no magical value (see John iv, 20 ff.).

His chief concern seems to have been to safeguard the shrine as 'a house of prayer' for all peoples (Mark xi, 17, citing Isaiah lxvi, 7). For this reason He cleared and cleansed the outer Court of the Gentiles of all the money-grubbing hucksters whose commerce and graft destroyed the sanctity of the holy place.

But there is a deeper reason for this action in His cleansing of the Temple Court, as Ernst Lohmeyer has noted with great perception.‡ Jesus came into the city in fulfilment of Old Testament prophecy (Mark xi, 1–11); and part of that fulfilment was His action in claiming the Temple for Himself, thus declaring Himself to be the rightful Lord of God's sanctuary. This is the meaning which Lohmeyer suggests for Mark xi, 11: 'And Jesus entered into Jerusalem, and into the temple.' He thus declared by this action that the prophetic expectation which Isaiah had foretold was now a present reality. This claim which He registered is summed up in Matthew xii, 6: 'But I say unto you, That in this place is one (literally,

* E. Stauffer, *Jesus and His Story* (London, E.T., 1960), pp. 93 ff.
† B. Gärtner, *John 6 and the Jewish Passover* (Lund, 1959), pp. 45 ff.
‡ E. Lohmeyer, *Lord of the Temple* (Edinburgh, E.T., 1961), pp. 34 f.

something) greater than the temple.' This is a veiled allusion to
the Kingdom which is a present reality in His person and
presence among men (Mark i, 15; Luke xi, 20). It follows from
this authoritative pronouncement that He is the true Lord of
the Temple that its worship is about to cease, as it is super-
seded by a new order. But our Lord speaks about this only
with poignancy and pathos as One who honoured all that was
best in the tradition of the ancestral faith and forms of worship
(Mark xiii, 2; xiv, 57–59), although He recognized the ways in
which an external religious devotion could prove a snare and
a spiritual danger (cf. Jeremiah vii – the whole chapter should
be read as a warning against a blind trust in religious ordinances).

Our Lord's Attitude

Jesus' attitude to the organized religion of His day, then, was
a twofold one. He valued the Temple, but chiefly for the facili-
ties it afforded for communion with God and for prayer more
than for its sacrificial apparatus. Yet in His own person He
embodied a new order which would eventually displace the
venerable cult of the holy place and the ceremonial offerings.
John iv, 21–24 is the fullest summary of His teaching on the
inwardness and reality of worship which is open to all who will
come 'in spirit and in truth' and available everywhere. But
there are many indications in the Synoptic Gospels that His
ministry and teachings were at variance with the cultic religion
of the Jewish leaders of His day; and that this conflict will lead
at length to a cross. Beyond the cross and broken body of the
Messiah there will be a new Body, the body of Christ, and a
new Temple (John ii, 19–22). These indications are seen in
such matters as His claim to forgive sins in His own right, His
refusal to fast, His disdain for the scribal Sabbath laws and for
those ritual taboos which made life so difficult and burdensome
for the common people of His day (Mark ii, 1–9, 15–17, 18–20
and 23 to iii, 6; vii, 1–23). We may also compare Luke xv,
1, 2; Matthew xxiii, 1–28; and in Matthew ix, 13 and xii, 7 He
justifies both His consorting with tax-collectors and sinners
whom the Pharisees specially despised, and His freedom to cut
through the scribal interpretation of the Sabbath regulation
on the ground of Hosea's prophecy: 'I desire mercy and not
sacrifice' (Hosea vi, 6; see also 1 Samuel xv, 22; Psalm li, 16;
Amos v, 21–24; Isaiah i, 10 ff. in similar vein).

It is not surprising that His followers adopted the same double attitude to the Temple cult. Peter and John go up to the Temple at the hour of prayer (Acts iii, 1), but there is no mention that they went to sacrifice there. Stephen proclaims the truth of the new Temple (Acts vi, 14 to vii, 50).* And the language of the New Testament in regard to sacrifice and offering is thoroughly spiritualized and sublimated with only occasional allusions to the Jewish calendar of fasts and festivals (Acts xx, 16; xxi, 17 ff.; 1 Corinthians xvi, 8. Contrast Colossians ii, 16, 17; Galatians iv, 10). The sacrifice which the Christian has to offer is the 'living sacrifice' of his person, yielded up in surrender and service for Christ. This is his 'reasonable worship' (Romans xii, 1, 2). The priestly office of the whole Church, (Revelation i, 6; v, 10, *etc.*) is no longer found at any earthly altar, for it is the offering of the sacrifice of praise and thanksgiving (Hebrews xiii, 15 with verse 10 possibly suggesting a reference to the Lord's Supper as a thanksgiving). The reason for this 'sublimation' is not far to seek. The sacrifice to end all atoning sacrifices has been offered on the altar of Calvary, and He who gave Himself, as both Priest and victim, can never again die (Romans vi, 9; Hebrews ix, 23–28), and has no need to officiate as though His once-offered work were inadequate (Hebrews x, 11 ff.). The sacrifices of good works (Hebrews xiii, 16), faith (Philippians ii, 17), evangelistic ministry (Romans xv, 16), almsgiving (Philippians iv, 18), and the martyr's courage (2 Timothy iv, 6) – these are the sacrifices which please God. The language of the Temple services and cultus remains – sacrifice, offering, priest, shrine are common terms. But it is reapplied to the Church's worship which is bound up with no earthly Temple and no human priestly mediation. The Church is the Spirit's shrine (1 Corinthians iii, 16, 17), a Temple not made with hands (Acts vii, 48; xvii, 24); and the worship the Church offers to God is essentially spiritual in character (John iv, 23–24; Philippians iii, 3, R.V.: 'for we . . . worship by the Spirit of God').

II. *The Worship of the Synagogue*

Our Lord's Galilean ministry was conducted in the open-air and in the synagogues of the districts He visited. He taught in the synagogues, and made it His regular practice to worship there on the Sabbath (Mark i, 21–28; iii, 1–6; vi, 2 f.; Matthew

* See R. Alan Cole, *The New Temple* (London, 1950).

iv, 23; Luke iv, 15, 16–30, 31 ff., 44; vi, 6; xiii, 10 ff.; John vi, 59; xviii, 20). St. Paul, in his missionary tours, made use of the synagogues of the Jewish Dispersion, i.e. the Jews who, while non-resident in the holy land, sought to be faithful to their ancestral faith. The record in Acts is particularly emphatic on this point (Acts xiii, 5; xiv, 1; xvii, 1; 10, 17; xviii, 4, 19). Nor was the Apostle alone in this practice of using the synagogue as a spring-board from which the Gospel message of Israel's hope and salvation might be sent forth to those who gathered as committed Jews or loosely attached 'God-fearers'; Apollos did exactly the same at Ephesus (Acts xviii, 26). It is clear that the Jewish synagogue was an important link in dissemination of the Good News and more than likely (as we observed earlier, p. 19) that its pattern of worship had a formative influence upon Christian worship.*

The Structure of Synagogue Worship

Jewish scholars have helped us to form a picture of the essential pattern of synagogue worship,† although it must be confessed that there are some matters which are debatable. For the period before the destruction of the Temple in A.D. 70 a most valuable source of information is contained in the New Testament (especially Luke iv, 15–21), but very few precise details are given in any contemporary document. But the general picture is tolerably clear.

There are three main elements: Praise, prayer and instruction.

Praise

It is the note of corporate praise which opens the service; and this is in accord with the principle laid down in the Talmud: 'Man should always first utter praises, and then pray.'‡ The adoption of this procedure may underlie the order

* The standard work on this indebtedness is C. W. Dugmore, *The Influence of the Synagogue upon the Divine Office* (Oxford, 1944). See, too, W. O. E. Oesterley, *The Jewish Background of the Christian Liturgy* (Oxford, 1925).

† Two straightforward accounts may be mentioned, apart from the more technical works: G. Dalman, *Jesus-Jeshua* (London, 1929) and P. P. Levertoff's essay on 'Synagogue Worship in the first century' in *Liturgy and Worship*, ed. W. K. L. Clarke (London, 1932).

‡ See *b. Berak.* 32a.

of 1 Corinthians xiv, 26 which bids that, at the head of the list
of Christian corporate worship at Corinth, 'a psalm' of praise
should be sung.

The 'ruler' summons the 'minister' (see Luke iv, 20) to invite someone from the congregation to commence the service
with this 'call to worship'. He begins with the cry: 'Bless ye the
Lord, the One who is to be blessed'; and the people respond
with the benediction: 'Blessed be the Lord . . . for ever,' in the
spirit of Nehemiah ix, 5. At the outset, then, the worshippers
are invited to think of God and to acknowledge His greatness
and blessing.

Prayers

Prayers in Jewish worship fall into two parts. The first group
comprise two lovely utterances (the *Yotzer* which means 'He
who forms' and takes up the theme of God as Creator of all
things; and the *'Ahabah* which means 'Love' and is concerned
both to recall God's love for His people and to pledge their
obligation to love Him in return. It ends: 'Blessed art Thou,
O Lord, who hast chosen Thy people Israel in love'). Immediately following these prayers comes the *Shema'* which is both
a confession of faith and a glad benediction. The title for the
Shema' derives from its opening word ('Hear' in Deuteronomy
vi, 4; 'Hear, O Israel, the Lord our God is one Lord'). As soon
as the congregation come to the word 'one' – for the *Shema'* is
recited antiphonally – the leader adds the glad ejaculation:
'Blessed be the name of the glory of His Kingdom for ever and
ever.' The term 'one' emphasizing the unity of God has always
been the central Jewish confession. It is given, therefore, a
special prominence in the liturgy; and we recall how Rabbi
Akiba died with this Hebrew word 'One' (*'ehad*) upon his
lips. In its full form the *Shema'* consists of Deuteronomy vi,
4–9; xi, 13–21; and Numbers xv, 37–41.

The second division of united prayer comes next, with the
way for it prepared by the reciting of the prayer known as
'True and firm' (is this word – the *Shema'* – to us for ever), with
its reminder that God's promises are sure and dependable to
His people. At this point, the 'minister' summons a member of
the assembly to lead in the 'Prayer proper', i.e. the Eighteen
Benedictions. The man so appointed steps forward in front of
the Ark and with his face turned towards the Ark, he leads the
united intercessions of the company who reply with Amen.

These 'Eighteen Blessings' cover a wide range of themes. They are partly an expression of praise, partly petitions for spiritual and material benefits and partly supplication for those in need (exiles, judges and counsellors and the chosen people). We may catch the tone of these prayers by considering the last one: 'Grant peace upon Israel Thy people and upon Thy city, and upon Thy inheritance, and bless us all together (lit. "as one"). Blessed art Thou O Lord, the Maker of peace.' It seems permissible to believe that these precise words were on the lips of Jesus as He entered, according to His custom, the synagogue for worship in His day.

Instruction

Once the prayers were said, the service assumed a form which has given to the synagogue its distinctive ethos. Indeed, the Jews themselves called it 'the house of instruction', for there is nothing more in keeping with Jewish worship than the emphasis which is placed upon Scripture-reading and exposition. Instruction was given by these two means. First, the Law and the Prophets were read by members of the congregation who came up and shared the task (according to the length of the portions involved). As the ancient Bible language of Hebrew was not understood by all present, a translator would turn the Scripture lessons into the vernacular, usually Aramaic. Then, there came the homily or address based on the passages read. Any person in the assembly who was considered suitable was invited to deliver this 'sermon' – as proved the case both at Nazareth (Luke iv, 21 ff.) and at Antioch (Acts xiii, 15 ff.). The service concluded with a blessing and the congregational Amen.

There were some modifications of this basic pattern, depending on the season of the year and the day of the week (Market days, Monday and Thursday, had shorter Scripture lections!). But the ingredients which provide the staple diet of synagogue worship – praise, prayer and instruction – are found in every case.

In our later chapters we shall see how these same elements are discovered in the New Testament patterns of worship, along with some distinctively Christian innovations. The evidence we shall look at will help us to see how well founded is the thesis that 'Christian worship, as a distinctive, indigenous thing, arose from the fusion, in the crucible of Christian experience, of the synagogue and the Upper Room. . . . The typical worship of the Church is to be found to this day in the union of the worship of the synagogue and the sacramental experience of the Upper Room; and that union dates from New Testament times'.*

* W. D. Maxwell, *An Outline of Christian Worship* (Oxford, 1945) p. 5.

3

The Prayers and Praises of the New Testament

Two types of prayer are known in the teaching and example of the New Testament Church. There is private prayer in the secret place of personal communion between the believer and his Lord. Much of the New Testament teaching deals directly with this aspect of Christian devotion, whether we think of the instructions of the Sermon on the Mount (Matthew vi, 5–8), or Jesus' parables on prayer (Luke xi, 5–13 and xviii, 1–14 are perhaps the best-known examples), or the many requests which the Apostle Paul makes that his friends should pray for him and his missionary service: 'ye also helping together by prayer for us' is his appeal to the Corinthians (2 Corinthians i, 11).

There are also the prayers of Jesus Himself, which are eloquent testimony to the reality and power of prayer and equally a guide and inspiration to us today in our prayer-life. A perceptive study of the prayer-life of Jesus will be found in James S. Stewart's book, *The Life and Teaching of Jesus Christ*; and this author shows how 'the praying Christ is the supreme argument for prayer'. Much guidance for Christian prayer can be obtained as we examine the occasions on which the Lord prayed and the content of those prayers. He prayed, we learn, at the critical moments of His life – at His baptism when His public ministry opened (Luke iii, 21); at the choosing of the Twelve (Luke vi, 12); at His transfiguration which followed the momentous challenge and response at Caesarea Philippi (Luke ix, 28); and at His agony in the Garden (Luke xxii, 39–45; Hebrews v, 7 also describes this scene). Indeed, He died – as He lived – praying (Luke xxiii, 46). From these episodes in the story of Jesus we gather that He sought the face of His Father at special times of crisis and need. But it is clear that communion with God was the daily inspiration of His life. Prayer, comments Professor Stewart, 'was not only an important part of His life: it *was* His life, the very breath of His being'.* And our Lord's prayers were far richer in content than a mere list of requests and preferences. Deep fellowship with God (Luke ix, 29); the exultation of thanksgiving (Luke x, 21 ff.) and an all-embracing intercession (Mark x, 16; Luke xxiii, 34; xxii, 31 f.; John xvii, 9) – these are the features of His life of prayer which set a standard for His disciples in all ages. For, in this respect as in some other ways, 'the disciple is not above his Lord' (John xiii, 16; xv, 20).

Those passages of the Gospel records which contain the actual words of Jesus in communion with God – Matthew xi, 25–27=Luke xi, 21, 22; Mark xiv, 36; John xvii – are worthy of our close attention, and will both inspire and direct our prayer-life as His modern disciples.

Corporate Prayer

But, in addition to the account of private prayer, there is the record of the Church's corporate prayer as the united assembly of believers voices its praise and supplication. And this aspect is our immediate concern as we consider the worship of the New Testament Church. Matthew xviii, 19–20 is perhaps the most well-known text in this connexion:

'Again I say unto you, That if two of you shall agree on earth as touching anything that they shall ask, it shall be done for them of my Father which is in heaven. For where two or three are gathered together in my name, there am I in the midst of them.'

This reference is to be understood in the light of a parallel from Rabbinical sources. Rabbi Hananiah said: 'If two sit together and the words of the Law (are spoken) between them, the divine Presence – the *Shekinah* – rests between them.'† For Christian believers, the Lord's promise is of a far richer presence and power. The two or three who are gathered (by Him) in His name, are assured that His living presence will be there. This is true in Sunday worship, and indeed whenever the Church meets to administer its life in accordance with the will of Christ (1 Corinthians v, 4). It is the other side

* J. S. Stewart, op. cit. (Edinburgh, 1933), p. 108.
† This 'saying' is taken from the Jewish 'The Sayings of the Fathers' (*Pirqe 'Aboth*) iii, 2 (Danby, *The Mishnah*, Oxford, 1933, p. 450). It is based on Malachi iii, 16.

of the dictum of Ignatius, the second century bishop and martyr: 'Wherever Jesus Christ is, there is the universal Church.'*

The Acts of the Apostles describes the prayer fellowship of the earliest believers. Acts ii, 42 refers to the practice of their corporate assembly, whether at home (ii, 46; iv, 23 ff.; v, 42) or in the Temple (iii, 1, 11; v, 12, 42). It is interesting to observe the circumstances which drew Christians together, and the thoughts which found expression in articulate prayer and praise. They needed and sought guidance (i, 14, 24). They came together under the duress of persecution and hostility (iv, 23–31), and requested the strengthening grace of their Lord to continue their witness for Him. They took the arrest and imprisonment of Peter (xii, 5) as a challenge to earnest intercession, for we should note that the real meaning of 'without ceasing' is 'fervently' (N.E.B.), literally 'in a stretched-out manner'; and God heard and answered, in spite of the wavering faith which hardly expected the divine intervention (xii, 12–17). They gathered at Antioch to worship the Lord, seeking the guidance which came in the Spirit's summons, 'Set apart Barnabas and Saul'; and with further united prayer these men who later hazarded their lives for the name of the Lord Jesus (xv, 26) were sent forth to the work of the Gospel in Asia Minor and the Christian mission was launched on its epoch-making way (xiii, 1–3). Other allusions to the united praying of the people of God are in xx, 36 and xxi, 5 – both touching scenes of tender pathos.

The Contents of Prayers and Praises

From the historical records there is little to guide us when we try to discover the contents of the prayers in the early Church. The prayers of the Church in Acts are *ad hoc* utterances, heartfelt praises and petitions called forth by the demands of the hour. Yet there are some important principles to be noted.

Acts i, 24. The object of this prayer, at the election of Matthias, is evidently God the Father, whom Luke regards as the sovereign disposer of human affairs and the guide of the Church's decisions.

Acts iv, 24–30. We may notice the invocation of God as 'sovereign', in verse 24 (cf. Luke ii, 29). In both texts the cor-

* *Smyrnaeans*, viii, 2.

responding term for the suppliant is 'servant'. In prayer the Jerusalem Church owned God as supreme Master. The title of Jesus, too, is 'servant' (verses 27, 30, R.V.), but a different Greek word is used, and may point to Isaiah's prophecy of the suffering Servant as the background. The use of the Psalter is important, as Christians instinctively, like their Lord (Luke xxiii, 46), turned to the Psalms of David for language in which to give vent to their deepest emotions. Perhaps in both cases the synagogue Liturgy was the abiding influence; and Psalm xxxi, 5 is a child's evening prayer in the Jewish home, corresponding to our 'Jesus, tender Shepherd, hear me.' Acts xiii, 1 f. is important because we learn from it that the Church at Antioch offered worship to the Lord. It is tempting to relate this to the worship of Jesus, a calling upon Him in devotion and supplication, as Stephen did (Acts vii, 59), and Paul too (2 Corinthians xii, 8). Many scholars find Christ-hymns (as in Philippians ii, 6–11; 1 Timothy iii, 16) in which Jesus is praised with a worship which belongs properly to God Himself. The phrase, 'calling upon the name of the Lord' (Acts ii, 21; ix, 14; xxii, 16; Romans x, 13 f.) points in the same direction for it seems to show that Jesus was hailed in worship as One worthy of adoration and surrender. It is likely that the phrase is borrowed from the Old Testament Scripture, where it denoted to 'practise the cult of Yahweh', 'to be a worshipper of . . . the true God' (Genesis iv, 26; xxi, 33, etc.). If this is so, nothing is more clearly shown than that Jesus was placed on a level with the covenant God by these Jewish Christians who only recently in the synagogue had confessed that God is one; and that right at the beginning of the Church age Jesus Christ was hailed with divine honours and placed at the centre of a cultus which drew its inspiration from His living presence in the midst of His own. A. M. Hunter in his finest book, *Paul and his Predecessors* has convincingly demonstrated that 'it is altogether likely that the primitive church worshipped Jesus as the exalted Messiah and Lord; that this presupposes a cultus (i.e. a properly religious devotion) of Christ; and that, in this confession and cultus of Jesus as the exalted Lord and Christ, lay the essential elements of all later Christology'.*

* A. M. Hunter, *Paul and his Predecessors* (second edition: London, 1961), p. 82. See too the detailed study of A. E. J. Rawlinson, *The New Testament Doctrine of the Christ* (London, 1926) and, for the worship of Jesus in the New Testament Church, J. M. Nielen, *The Earliest Christian Liturgy* (London, E. T., 1941).

On the last point in Professor Hunter's statement it is interesting to

We shall take up this matter in the following chapter.
There is one piece of evidence which is of considerable
interest and value. At the close of 1 Corinthians we read the
strange-sounding Aramaic term *Maranatha* (xvi, 22) which our
English translations render as either 'our Lord cometh' (R.V.
margin) or 'our Lord, come!' (R.S.V.). It seems fairly certain
that the second alternative is to be preferred and that this
phrase is a prayer of invocation, addressed to Jesus. Similar
language is found in Revelation xxii, 20: 'Even so, come, Lord
Jesus', and the Church Order known as *The Teaching of the
Twelve Apostles* (or *Didache*) uses the exact formula for a
service preparatory to the Lord's table. The precise setting of
the words at the end of 1 Corinthians is disputed,* but it is
more important to recognize from this prayer to the risen Lord
the way in which He is hailed and worshipped. The use of an
Aramaic phrase can only be satisfactorily explained on the
assumption that *Marana tha* is an ancient watchword which
takes us back to the earliest days of the Church in Palestine
where Aramaic was the spoken language, for we can hardly
imagine why St. Paul would trouble to include a term (in
what was to the Corinthian believers a foreign tongue) in a
Letter written to those who spoke and understood Greek unless, in fact, *Marana tha* had become accepted as a liturgical
term from the earliest days of the Church. Today we freely use
a word like *Amen* in prayer without stopping to recall that *we*
are employing an ancient Hebrew term. *Marana tha* had become an accepted part of the Corinthians' religious vocabulary
as *Amen* (= 'Let it be so') has become part of ours.
Now the evidence of this ancient Christian invocation to
Christ throws a flood of light on the way in which the Jewish-
Christians worshipped their Lord. For not only is *Marana tha*
the oldest Christian prayer of which we have record;[†] it can

* See C. F. D. Moule, *Worship in the New Testament* (London, 1961),
pp. 43 f.

† So A. Hamman, *La Prière: Le Nouveau Testament* (Tournai, 1959),
p. 276.

note Philippians ii, 5–11 in which the enthroned Christ is hailed as Lord
and to recall J. Jeremias' similar conclusion about this passage: 'As this
Christ-hymn is pre-Pauline, it is the oldest evidence for . . . the teaching
of the three levels of Christ's existence' (i.e. pre-existent, incarnate and
exalted). This teaching, he avers, was basic for the developed Christology
of later times. Art. 'Zur Gedankenführung in den paulinischen Briefen,'
Studia Paulina (ed. J. N. Sevenster and W. C. van Unnik: Haarlem,
1953), p. 154.

only mean that those who only lately had invoked the name of their covenant God as 'Lord' in the synagogue Liturgy now came to apply the same divine title to Jesus the Messiah. Long before the Church had begun to speculate about the Trinitarian formulas in which its later creeds were to be defined, it was confessing that Jesus was one with God and was worthy of such divine and transcendent honours as most properly belonged to the one, true and living God, the Maker of heaven and earth. Christology was born in the atmosphere of worship.

Corporate Prayer in the Epistles

We are not left in doubt that the first communities of Christian people called upon the name of their risen Lord as they met to worship. As a frontispiece to the first Corinthian letter Paul reminds the Church (in 1 Corinthians i, 2) that they are united with all the other assemblies in the world which 'call upon the name of' a common Lord. The phrase used in this verse implies a public invocation of Jesus and a profession of faith in Him as the exalted Head of His people. But have we any examples of the sort of prayer and praise which was offered to Him?

It is true that no objective description of an early Christian service of worship exists. Perhaps the nearest we get to that is the account of Paul's visit to Troas (Acts xx, 7–12). Yet it seems clear that Paul had before his mind's eye, as he wrote his Letters or dictated them to his amanuenses, a picture of the Church assembled for public worship. The introductory greetings and opening prayers of thanksgiving are couched in no commonplace language but reflect, by their fullness of expression and unusual vocabulary, the liturgical life of the Churches. The passage in Ephesians i, 3–14 is a good illustration of this. About this notable section three things may be said:

(i) The Apostle's thought is extended and carried forward from one theme to another by the use of relative clauses. It is this fact which makes a public reading of Ephesians i so difficult and breathtaking!

(ii) The sentences are not only rhythmical but have a marked euphony which gives a sonorous lilt to the words when they are read out in the original Greek.

(iii) The section may be divided into stanzas, corresponding to our verses 3–6; 7–12; 13–14. In each stanza there is the refrain 'to the praise of his glory' (in verses 6, 12, 14) which comes at the end of the strophe and gives to it a fitting conclusion.

It is therefore with sure instinct that scholars have detected in this magnificent outburst of the personal prayer of the Apostle liturgical phrases and terms which he borrows from the worship of God's people. They are the common property of the Church as it reflects upon the love of God, the redemption of Christ and the working of the Holy Spirit in human lives.

There is yet another line of evidence. From 1 Corinthians v, 1 ff. we learn that Paul regards himself as no detached and impartial observer of the life of his converts. In a solemn mood he enjoins what must be done at Corinth as though he himself were personally present in the congregation. Indeed, he *is* present in their midst (verse 4) as he shares with them in spiritual communion. That this is no isolated incident occasioned by the seriousness of the situation at Corinth is seen by Colossians ii, 5: 'For though I be absent in the flesh, yet am I (present) with you in the spirit, joying and beholding your order.' Thus his reported prayers may be the shared possession of all his Churches.

And, then, we know that his letters were intended to be read out in public services (Colossians iv, 16; 1 Thessalonians v, 27); and as this was done, he would invite his readers to be his fellow-worshippers and join with him in an exercise of heart devotion and praise. The clearest example of the language of prayer into which Paul lapses as he pens his epistles is found in Ephesians iii, 14 ff. Here again we may notice the long sentences and elevated thoughts; and at the climax comes the splendid doxology of verses 20, 21:

'Now unto him that is able to do exceeding abundantly above all that we ask or think, according to the power that worketh in us. Unto him be glory in the Church by Christ Jesus throughout all ages, world without end. Amen.'

Some Special Words for Prayer

We turn to consider some unusual expressions which found a place in the prayer-speech of the early believers.

(i) *'Abba* suggests our Lord's Gethsemane prayer, recorded in Mark xiv, 32–39: ''Abba, Father, all things are possible unto thee.' As was the case with *Marana tha* in 1 Corinthians xvi, 22, this Aramaic word recurs in its original form in Paul's

Greek letters: at Romans viii, 15 and Galatians iv, 6; and is translated for the benefit of the first readers. It seems certain therefore that *'Abba* was current coin in the early Churches as a title for God of special significance and depth of meaning. And such can be shown to be very probable once we examine the precise sense of this word.

'Abba is our Lord's favourite designation for God; and has been the subject of much scholarly research.* We have the German scholars to thank for the conclusion that while *'Abba* was the child's word for his earthly father, there is no evidence that the pious Jew ever used precisely this form (meaning 'dear father', 'daddy') of God. Instead, he used a variant form like *'Abinu,* 'our Father'), but *'Abba* was avoided because it was thought to be too daring and familiar an expression to be used of the King of the Universe. Now, God's Son uses exactly this homely expression, which perhaps is not surprising since from His early boyhood He was conscious of a unique filial relationship with God (Luke ii, 49). The staggering thing is that He teaches His disciples to do the same. This leads us to the so-called Lord's Prayer, recorded in Matthew vi, 9–13 and Luke xi, 2–4. We should notice at once that it is more the disciples' prayer than the Lord's, but the title is now part of our speech and may be justified on the ground that it was the Lord who gave this prayer to His people in response to the request, 'Lord, teach us to pray.' There is evidence to show that very early in the Church's history this prayer became accepted as a pattern prayer and was backed by dominical authority. As early as the time when the *Didache* was compiled as a manual of Church order and practice (say, A.D. 80–100), this prayer had become an integral part of Christian worship: 'And do not pray as the hypocrites, but as the Lord commanded in His Gospel, pray thus . . . three times a day' (*Didache* viii). It was intended to be said corporately, 'when *ye* pray, say', as Cyprian pointed out in a later century; and Tertullian (*c.* A.D. 150–225) speaks of 'common prayers and united supplications', probably with the Lord's Prayer in mind.†

As to the contents of the prayer, we may observe, with T. W.

* For the discussion on the meaning of *'Abba,* see *Theological Dictionary of the New Testament*, Vol. I. (Grand Rapids, 1964), pp. 5 f.

† The difference in wording is best explained (with J. Jeremias, *The Sermon on the Mount* (London, E.T., 1961), p. 22) by the different audiences envisaged. In Matthew it is a Jewish-Christian audience, whereas the Lukan version is a Gentile-Christian instruction in prayer.

Manson,* that they 'fall into two main divisions, the first concerned with what may be called world issues, the second with the affairs of individuals. Both alike are conceived as being in the hands of the Father: the same God who orders the course of history with sovereign power also ministers to the daily needs, material and spiritual, of his individual children.'

The range of the prayer should also be noticed, extending from the highest aspirations of which the human emotion and will is capable ('May Thy name be sanctified, Thy Kingdom come, Thy will be done in the world – and by me') to the humblest need ('Give us today the bread for the coming day'). The prayer 'reveals God as concerned with things infinitely great and infinitely little' and shows that 'the will of the Father covers the whole life of man: and the whole man may enter into communion with the Father'. It is the sum of Jesus' teaching on the Fatherhood of God; and if men desire to learn what this means, it is the Lord's Prayer that will show them.

While the Prayer is not referred to as such in the New Testament Epistles, it cannot be accidental that Paul frequently begins his prayers for the Churches by invoking the name of God as Father. He prays to the Father of Jesus Christ – and so by implication, the Father of all who are bound to Christ in the one family of His grace (see Romans viii, 15–17). And it is surely significant that in this paragraph Paul uses the Aramaic term *'Abba* (as in Galatians iv, 6) to highlight the spirit of filial adoption which becomes ours as the Holy Spirit witnesses to our membership of the family of God. It may even be that *'Abba* in these texts (as in 1 Peter i, 17) is a veiled allusion to the Lord's Prayer, the meaningful saying of which brought to the newly-born convert a deep awareness of joyful privilege that he belonged to God's family. This would then explain the following reference in 1 Peter to 'newborn babes' (1 Peter ii, 2).

(ii) *Amen* is a familiar Christian term. In the synagogue worship, as in the Old Testament, it was the people's full-hearted and full-throated ('the sound of a grand Amen') response to and endorsement of the words of another (e.g., Nehemiah viii, 6). The word means literally 'to be firm, true', and is connected with the verb 'to believe'. It occurs most ob-

---

* T. W. Manson, *The Teaching of Jesus* (Cambridge, 1931), p. 113. His treatment (pp. 113 ff.) is especially valuable as the following one or two sentences above show. For a more recent and suggestive devotional study, see W. Lüthi, *The Lord's Prayer* (Edinburgh, E.T., 1961).

viously at the close of the New Testament doxologies which ascribe praise to God and His Christ (Romans i, 25; ix, 5; xi, 36; xvi, 27; Galatians i, 5; Ephesians iii, 21; Philippians iv, 20; 1 Timothy i, 17; vi, 16; 2 Timothy iv, 18; Hebrews xiii, 21; 1 Peter iv, 11; v, 11; Jude 25. Revelation v portrays a dramatic scene, and probably reflects the worship of the Church militant as well as the Church triumphant in heaven. The response of the living creatures to the acclamation of the angels is 'Amen' as they who represent (with the elders) the whole of redeemed creation add their witness to and approval of the universal paean, 'To Him that sits upon the throne, and to the Lamb, be blessing and honour and glory and power, for ever and ever' (verses 13, 14).

Two other passages are full of interest. 2 Corinthians i, 20 f. pictures a scene which most likely takes us back to early worship. Christ, avers the Apostle, confirms to us the promises of God, and our fitting response to God's faithfulness in His Word is the *Amen* which accepts and endorses all that God has promised in the Gospel. 'That is why, when we give glory to God, it is through Christ Jesus that we say "Amen" . . . it is God who has set his seal upon us, and as a pledge of what is to come has given the Spirit to dwell in our hearts' (N.E.B.). The liturgical terminology of the whole passage is especially rich, and quite possibly Paul is alluding to the rite of Christian baptism under the figure of the 'seal'. The latter became a descriptive word in the Church for the work of the Holy Spirit who, in baptism, imparted an assurance of divine sonship to the converts.

In 1 Corinthians xiv, 16 Paul rebukes the Church for their unbridled indulgence in the more exotic 'gifts of the Spirit' in public assembly. He is concerned lest an uninstructed person, an 'outsider', should come into the Church meeting and be embarrassed by a display of strange speech. 'How then will he be able to add his Amen to your thanksgiving when he does not know what you are saying?' asks the Apostle, thus making it clear that *Amen* was in common use as the worshipper's assent to what he heard from the lips of his fellow-believers.

(iii) The same verse quoted above (1 Corinthians xiv, 16) also contains a reference to the prayer of 'thanksgiving'. The presence of the definite article *'the* thanksgiving' seems to suggest that a particular type of praying is envisaged, as distinct from the general use of the term 'to give thanks' (as in 2 Corinthians i, 11; ix, 12; 1 Thessalonians v, 18). Little is said about the content of such a Thanksgiving prayer. It is possible that the prayer at the Lord's table is in mind; and we shall see later that it is this verb (Greek: *eucharistein* – 'to give thanks') which has given the name Eucharist to the Lord's Supper as an occasion when, in a pre-eminent way, the Christian Church offers praise and thankful acknowledgement of the blessings of redemption in Christ. Nevertheless, in the Pastoral letters, we read of such Thanksgiving prayers which are not connected with the Lord's table – in 1 Timothy ii, 1 and iv, 4, 5. The last-mentioned is particularly significant for it hints at a thanksgiving over food.

Our Lord, in the Gospels, always blessed God before a meal and offered thanks afterward (Mark vi, 41; viii, 6; xiv, 22 f.; Luke xxiv, 30; John vi, 11, 23). This was in accord with the Jewish custom which attached considerable importance to 'grace before meals' which both acknowledged God as Creator and Provider of food and 'consecrated' the food on the table for human consumption.* Paul likewise accepts the truth of God as the Giver of all good (1 Corinthians x, 26 quoting Psalm xxiv, 1: 'The earth is the Lord's') but, catching the spirit of his Lord (in Mark vii, 1–19), refuses to allow the elaborate distinctions between 'clean' and 'unclean' meats – a prominent theme of Rabbinical discussion† – to rob him or the Church of the benefit of God's creation (1 Timothy iv, 4, 5). The only thing which could do that would be an ungrateful and unthinking acceptance of food. But to take it 'with thanksgiving' means that we may surely 'eat and drink' to the glory of God (1 Corinthians x, 31).

Further prayers of gratitude to God and His Son are scattered throughout the book of Revelation. The seer, caught up in the Spirit on the Lord's day (i, 10), records the visions he saw of the heavenly host who worship God unceasingly (iv, 8). But the language he uses is that of the Church upon earth; and in xi, 16–18 we may overhear something of the hymns of worship and thanksgiving which are offered:

> 'We give thanks to thee, Lord God almighty,
>   who art and who wast,
>   that thou has taken thy great power and hast
>   begun to reign.'

* The tractate *Berakoth* ('Blessings') in the Mishnah deals with these matters. See, too, G. A. Michell's discussion, *Eucharistic Consecration in the Primitive Church* (London, 1948).
† See the tractate '*Abodah Zarah* ('Strange Worship') in the Mishnah.

4

Hymns and Spiritual Songs

The Christian Church was born in song. The proof of this statement may be adduced along a number of different lines. First of all, it is to be expected that the Christian Gospel should bring with it on the scene of history an outburst of hymnody and praise to God. Then, it may be argued that all the antecedents of the Church's appearance in the world of the first century would lead us also to expect that the early Church will be a hymn-singing community. And, thirdly, we may investigate the New Testament books with a view to discerning therein the presence of, or witness to, such canticles of worship.

I. That the Gospel of God should be attended by an upsurge of spiritual fervour and power is what we might anticipate from our understanding of the ways of God with men, and indeed from our knowledge of ourselves. For the Gospel of the Apostolic age was not a theological theorem, presented in a cold, detached and impersonal way, to be accepted with all the unfeeling and nonchalant reserve with which a student of mathematics learns his lessons! Indeed, Archimedes with his enthusiastic cry of *Eureka* – 'I've found it' – is the great exception. The preaching of the Good News and its reception by faith were both heart-moving and rapturously joyous experiences; and we have only to read the early chapters in Acts to be persuaded of this fact (see Acts ii, 1–13, 47; iii, 8; v, 41, 42; viii, 39; xiii, 52). St. Paul captures this note of 'the conquering new-born joy'* of the first Christians when he writes to the Church at Rome: 'The kingdom of God is . . . righteousness, peace and *joy in the Holy Spirit*' (Romans xiv, 17). No fruit of the Spirit was more characteristic of the early Church than the possession and display of joy in the Lord (Galatians

---

* For this aspect of the New Testament Church-life, see **P. G. S.** Hopwood, *The Religious Experience of the Primitive Church* (Edinburgh, 1936).

v, 22; Philippians iv, 4); and believers would hardly have understood Swinburne's mournful lines: 'Thou hast conquered, O pale Galilean; the world has grown grey from Thy breath.'

And that this spiritual energy and verve, newly released by the Pentecostal Spirit, should give expression in songs of praise is again a natural consequence. A. B. Macdonald makes this point when he writes: * '*A priori*, we should expect that a movement which released so much emotion, and loyalty, and enthusiasm, would find expression in Song.' After quoting cases of religious awakening in the history of the Church in later years (such as the eighteenth century Revival) and showing that these have been accompanied by outbursts of song, he goes on: 'So it would have been strange indeed if the Church had remained songless in that first glorious dawn when the light from Christ came breaking across the horizons, making all things new.'

II. But Christian song did not break forth upon a world which had been hitherto dumb and in which hymns were unknown. The Church was cradled in Judaism, and borrowed many of its forms of worship from the Temple and synagogue.† Antiphonal singing goes back to the pre-exilic period of Jewish history (Exodus xv, 21; Numbers x, 35 f.; xxi, 17; 1 Samuel xviii, 7). Many of the Psalms were intended to be sung in the congregational worship of the Temple (e.g., Psalms xxiv, cxviii, cxxxiv, cxlv). The data from the post-exilic age indicate a well-ordered arrangement for responsive singing between two choirs of musicians (Ezra iii, 11: 'and they sang responsively, praising and giving thanks to the Lord'; Nehemiah xii, 24; 31). In the century before the coming of Christ, hymnic worship was developed by the sect of the Therapeutae whom Philo describes.‡ At their meetings, one of the company stands up and 'sings a hymn to God, either a new one which he has himself composed, or an old one by an earlier composer. The others follow one by one in fitting order, while all listen in complete silence, except when they have to sing

* A. B. Macdonald, *Christian Worship in the Primitive Church* (Edinburgh, 1934) p. 112.
 † The Old Testament and Jewish setting of New Testament patterns of musical worship have been fully described and discussed by W. S. Smith, *Musical Aspects of the New Testament* (Amsterdam, 1962).
 ‡ Philo, *Vit. Cont.*, chapters 80 ff.

the refrains and responses'. At the night-time services, the men and women are at first separated. All in both groups sing hymns, some parts antiphonally, and these anthems are accompanied by certain rhythmical movements of the body. Then, 'divinely inspired, the men and women together, having become one choir' sing 'hymns of thanks to the Saviour God'.

The community of the Dead Sea scrolls similarly had musical features in their worship. For instance, the Essene scribe writes thus: *

> 'I will sing with knowledge and all my music
> Shall be for the glory of God.
> (My) lyre (and) my harp shall sound
> For His holy order
> And I will tune the pipe of my lips
> To His right measure' (*The Community Rule*, x. 9).

In the Thanksgiving Hymns of the Qumran community the language is that of an individual's gratitude to God for His mercies, and a series of Hymns opens with the words: 'I thank Thee, O Lord', or 'I thank Thee, my God'. The poet, who *may* be the famous Teacher of Righteousness of the sect, acknowledges the goodness of God in this way:

> 'What am I . . .
>   that Thou shouldst lay hymns of thanksgiving
> within my mouth,
> And (praise) upon my tongue?'
>
> (*The Hymns*, xi. 3, 4).

When we come to look at the immediate background to the New Testament in the practices of normative Judaism (that is, the Judaism of the Rabbis), we admit that there is some doubt as to the extent to which the singing of divine praises had developed in the Palestinian synagogues of the first century.† It is probable that the synagogues of the Dispersion – the exiled Jews who lived and worked outside the holy land – were more advanced than their more conservative Palestinian

* The texts are taken from the Pelican book translation of G. Vermès, *The Dead Sea Scrolls in English* (London, 1962).

† There is an important background of Christian hymnology in the ancient Greek world. For some discussion about this and for details concerning Jewish hymn-singing, see the writer's article, 'Aspects of Worship in the New Testament Church', *Vox Evangelica* ii (London, 1963), pp. 7 ff.

brethren in the use of psalmody. But there can be no doubt that the early believers in Jesus inherited the desire to express their gratitude to God in the offering of vocal praises, as the Lord Himself had done (Matthew xxvi, 30 which is a reference to the *Hallel* psalm of the Passover festival). Moreover, there were ready to hand the Old Testament psalms which the early Church took over, as we can see from the use which was made of the Psalms in the prayers in Acts and in the theological discussions in Hebrews (which some scholars place in a liturgical context), especially chapters i, ii.*

The Old Testament hymn-book of the Psalter was read with Christian eyes, and prefigurations and prophecies of Christ were quickly detected. We may hold that, with the Master's encouragement of Luke xxiv, 44: 'All things which were written in the law of Moses, and in the prophets, and in the psalms, concerning me' to guide them, the Christian teachers and preachers would naturally turn to the Scriptures for inspiration and direction – indeed we know that the earliest apologetic was undertaken to show that the events of the Cross and Resurrection happened 'according to the Scriptures' (1 Corinthians xv, 3 ff.). And the first prayers of the Church in Acts are based upon the Psalms of David (especially Acts iv, 24–30). Another sign we have that the Psalter was used to express Christian worship is in the Apocalypse of John. Some of the hymns he reports are fashioned as a mosaic of Old Testament quotations. Of Revelation xv, 3, 4, A. Hamman says†: 'The canticle (in these verses) is a *cento* of Biblical reminiscences, borrowed principally from the Psalter':

'Great and marvellous are Thy works,
Lord God Almighty,
Just and true are Thy ways,
Thou King of the nations!
Who shall not fear Thee, O Lord,
And glorify Thy name?
For Thou only art holy;
For all nations shall come and worship before Thee;
For Thy judgments are made manifest.'

* See, on the use of the Old Testament in the letter to the Hebrews, *The Psalm Citations in the Epistle to the Hebrews* by S. Kistemaker (Amsterdam, 1961).

† A. Hamman, *La Prière: Le Nouveau Testament*, p. 367.

As we shall see later, it is likely that the Pauline allusions in Colossians iii, 16 and Ephesians v, 19 to 'psalms' reflect the use of Christian compositions – and this conclusion is to be drawn mainly on the ground that the adjective 'spiritual' (or more precisely, 'inspired by the Spirit') in the latter part of these texts goes with the term 'psalms' also. It is not likely, therefore, that Paul would speak of 'psalms inspired by the Spirit's afflatus' if he intended the reference to be to the borrowing of traditional odes from the hymn-book of the Jewish Psalter. Compositions which were spontaneously 'inspired' and created for the occasion are much more probably in view, as in the situation described in 1 Corinthians xiv. But the allusion in James v, 13: 'Is any merry? Let him sing psalms' may be taken to refer to Davidic psalms. There is no means of knowing the genre of the hymns which Paul and Silas sang in the Philippian jail, but if we are correct in reasoning that the human spirit, under duress and trial, turns instinctively to what is familiar and well-known, there is then nothing to deny that the Psalms of the Old Testament rang through the dark prison, greatly to the interest of the missionaries' fellow-captives.

There is yet one further section of the New Testament literature where the influence of the Old Testament lyrical writing is in evidence: this is the Nativity and Infancy preface to Luke's Gospel. Four canticles in these two chapters (Luke i, ii) have a distinct poetic form and may be arranged in strophes as a species of early Christian hymnody which takes us back to the Jewish-Christian Church. The Old Testament colouring of the vocabulary is unmistakable. The passages are:

(i) Luke i, 46–55. This passage contains the hymn known to Christian worship as the *Magnificat* from the opening word of the Vulgate translation in verse 46: 'My soul *doth magnify the Lord*'. The speaker is Mary who 'celebrates in an exalted poetic strain the now certain coming of the Messiah'.* Her anthem is dependent upon the model of Hannah's song (in 1 Samuel i, 11; ii, 1–10), and the style is patterned upon a parallelism and use of couplets which enables us to see a possible four-fold division (verses 46–48; 49, 50; 51–53; 54, 55). To be sure, there is an absence of any specifically Christian ideas, as distinct from pre-Christian aspirations and yearnings; but later Christian worship has found in these stately words, when transposed into a full Christian key, a sublime confession of the faithfulness of God to His servants.

* W. Manson, *The Gospel according to Luke* (London, 1930), p. 12.

(ii) The Psalm of Zachariah, in Luke i, 68–79, is called the *Benedictus* from the opening Latin word of the Vulgate text. It falls into two parts, and may be subdivided into five strophes as follows:

(*a*) verses 68, 69; 70–72; 73–75.

(*b*) verses 76, 77; 78, 79.

The first part, comprising verses 68–75, is cast in a Jewish mould in much the same way as the *Magnificat*. B. S. Easton comments:* 'The concept of redemption is much the same as in the *Magnificat*, but with greater emphasis on the ceremonial worship.' The aged priest rejoices in the promised mercy of God by which national deliverance from the power of Rome will be secured (verse 71), although the emancipation will be effected through spiritual means. The thought continues in the pledge of service and allegiance to God (verse 75). With verse 76, however, the second part begins, and it is at this point that a distinctively Christian note is sounded. The task of the newly-born life is clearly depicted (verse 76 f.), and John's great work is described in such a way as to recall the Jewish expectation of the Elijah who was awaited as the precursor of Messiah (Malachi iv, 5–6).

(iii) Two shorter hymnic tributes are found in Luke ii. The *Gloria in excelsis* (in ii, 14) is a memorable statement of angelic jubilation at the coming of the Redeemer:

'To God in the highest, glory!
To His people on earth, peace! '

It is not surprising that this paean of praise quickly found a place in the Church's corporate worship, and became a regular feature of its morning worship, according to the fourth century *Apostolic Constitutions* which was an early Church Order.

(iv) The same *Apostolic Constitutions* also speaks of the *Nunc Dimittis* ('Lord, now lettest Thou Thy servant depart in peace') of the venerable Simeon as an evening hymn of Church liturgy; and it is easy to see how its structure is made up of three component parts (in verse 29; verses 30, 31; verse 32).

As we look back on these ancient expressions of Jewish-Christian piety and expectation which awaited the coming of the Deliverer (see Luke ii, 25 and 38), we catch something of the spirit of yearning and hope which they breathe. The Christian knows that God answered these aspirations in a way far

* B. S. Easton, *Commentary on the Gospel of Luke* (London, 1926), ad loc.

more wonderful than these pietists could have imagined; and so it is perfectly legitimate and spiritually profitable for such anthems and versicles to have found a place in the liturgical life of the later Church. The reminders of God's never-failing mercy and covenant-faithfulness in the advent of Christ and His Kingdom are truths which form an integral part of our faith, and of such truths these hymns so eloquently speak.

III.   So far we have been concerned with the use of hymns and psalms which the early Church took over from the Temple and synagogue worship or with such forms as were adapted by the Christians from these sources. In the latter category may be placed also parts of the book of Revelation which seem to be borrowed directly from the synagogues of the Greek-speaking Jewish world (passages such as Revelation iv, 11; xi, 17, 18; xiv, 7;, xv, 3, 4). The most illustrious of these examples, however, is an ejaculation which has secured for itself a firm niche in the language of Christian praise. From the opening words of Revelation iv, 8, it is known as the *Ter sanctus* – the 'Thrice Holy':

> 'Holy, holy, holy, is the Lord God Almighty,
> Who was and is and is to come.'

What is true of this section characterizes the entire group of Jewish-Christian fragments. The praise they offer is to the holy and righteous God of Judaism who is extolled (as we have seen earlier) in the synagogue Liturgy as Creator and Sustainer of the world, and Judge of all. The introductory phrases which the seer of Revelation uses are interesting. The verses are prefaced by such terms as: 'they never ceased to sing'; 'singing'; 'the elders fell down on their faces and worshipped God, saying'; 'he said with a loud voice'; 'they sing the song of Moses'. All this suggests that the writer, the seer John whom Christian tradition names as 'the liturgist',* sought to set forth his depictions of the heavenly scene and the celestial worship by projecting on to his canvas the forms and patterns which belonged to his knowledge of the worship of the Church on earth. For this feature there is a precedent, for it is known that later

---

* E. Stauffer, *New Testament Theology* (London, E.T., 1955), pp. 40, 202 shows beyond all doubt the liturgical and cultic setting of much of the imagery of the Apocalypse. The name 'liturgist' goes back as far as to Chrysostom (*Or.* 36). See further W. Milligan, *The Revelation of St. John* (London, 1887), p. 287.

Judaism was familiar with the idea of the inter-relation of heavenly and earthly cultus.* There are texts which speak of liturgical songs in heaven, but the language belongs to Jewish worship on the earth. It is certainly understandable that the Christian seer should resort to this practice of using the forms and cadre which were taken from his own experience. How else could he have made his descriptions intelligible to his readers?

To the same group of Jewish-Christian fragments of hymnic praise belong such verses as Romans xi, 33–35 and 1 Timothy i, 17. The last-named ascription is addressed to 'the King of the ages, immortal, invisible, the only God'. The first designation of God as 'King of the ages' is exactly the phrase used at Jewish table-prayers ('Blessed be Thou, O Lord our God, King of the Ages') and in synagogue praise. It is used very frequently when the name of God is blessed, in order to lend dignity and deference to the benediction. As He is the immortal God, it is fitting that honour and glory should be His 'for ever and ever', and this is a Greek expression which helps to anchor the doxology of 1 Timothy in the Church life of some Greek-speaking Hebrew Christian community. Jeremias' verdict seems sound when he calls it 'a liturgical Prayer-formula which the Church often prayed in worship and which is derived from the Prayer-treasury of the pre-Christian, Hellenistic synagogue'.† To a similar source we should trace the doxology also of 1 Timothy vi, 15, 16.

Now our attention is directed to what are specifically and distinctively Christian compositions. Are there traces of such Christian hymns to be found within the pages of the New Testament? Certain texts will dispose us to answer that question with a 'Yes'.

1 Corinthians xiv, 26 gives the injunction for the assembly at Corinth: 'When you come together (for public worship) each one of you has a hymn, a lesson, a revelation, a tongue or an interpretation.' Added to this piece of evidence for the existence of Christian hymns is 1 Corinthians xiv, 15 which looks forward to the reference to the 'hymn' in verse 26. May it be that the placing of the term 'hymn' at the head of the list indicates that the service at Corinth began with a hymn? If so,

---

* Cf. *Test. Levi* 3; *Enoch* xx, 4; *Ascension of Isaiah*, ix, 5; and in the New Testament, Hebrews xii, 22; 2 Corinthians xii, 4.

† J. Jeremias, *Die Briefe an Timotheus und Titus* (Göttingen, 1953), p. 13.

it would link up with the synagogue order, which also commences with the note of praise.

Colossians iii, 16 and Ephesians v, 19, 20 go together, and tell us of the existence of 'psalms and hymns and spiritual songs'. It is hard to draw any hard-and-fast distinction between these terms; and modern scholars are agreed that the various terms are used loosely to cover the various forms of musical composition. 'Psalms' may refer to Christian odes patterned on the Old Testament psalter. 'Hymns' would be longer compositions and there is evidence that some actual specimens of these hymns may be found in the New Testament itself. 'Spiritual songs', refer to snatches of spontaneous praise which the inspiring Spirit placed on the lips of the enraptured worshipper, as I Corinthians xiv, 15 implies. These 'inspired odes' would no doubt be of little value, and their contents would be quickly forgotten.

At this point one may ask for the standards by which any particular portion of the New Testament may be pronounced as hymnic in form and style. This inquiry would take us into a technical discussion, the gist of which may be read in another place.* The best solution will be to consider some of the most likely 'hymnic' sections of the New Testament, and observe how the principles which should be borne in mind when it comes to a classification of New Testament hymns are to be applied to actual cases.

Ephesians v, 14 is usually regarded as the most cogent example of early Christian hymnology. And there are good grounds for this confidence. The introductory words, 'Wherefore it says' read as though they were added expressly to prepare for the citation of a familiar passage, well known to Paul's readers. The verse naturally falls into three lines on the grounds of style, with a swinging trochaic rhythm in the Greek and the employment of a rhetorical device by which the first two lines end with the same sound. A translation runs:

> 'Awake, O sleeper,
> From thy grave arise.
> The light of Christ upon thee shines.'

As a whole the verse contains an invocational appeal addressed to the Christian and summoning him to action. At

---

* In the author's article, *Vox Evangelica* ii (London, 1963) pp. 16 ff. Bibliographical references to the following paragraphs in the text above will be found in this article.

the same time it offers him the promise of Divine favour and
aid. The first two lines are a rousing summons to moral
activity; and the third line is the accompanying promise of
God.

In view of these contents, couched in the language of exhortation and using a combination of metaphors (sleep, death,
light) applied to the spiritual life of the Christian at his conversion and entry into the Church's fellowship, the most
natural event with which the verse is to be associated is Christian baptism.* The lines would then be the accompanying
chant to the actions of the baptismal service when the believer
was buried in the water with Christ and raised again to newness of life (Romans vi, 4 ff; Colossians ii, 12); and this leads
one commentator on the text to submit that such a verse as
Ephesians v, 14 would be fixed indelibly upon the heart and
mind of the convert as he emerged from the baptismal water.
Paul recalls it in his appeal to the Ephesian Christians, just as
a preacher today might reinforce a point by the citation of
the verse of a well-known and loved hymn.

Those features which make Ephesians v, 14 stand out from
its context are to be found in other places also. Scholars have
looked for passages which have a lyrical quality and rhythmical style, an unusual vocabulary which is different from the
surrounding context of the letter in which the passage appears,
some distinctive piece of Christian doctrine (usually associated
with the Person and work of our Lord Jesus Christ) and hints
that the passage in question finds its natural setting in a baptismal or Communion service. From these features it is
possible to identify and classify with a reasonable degree of
accuracy and certainty the following New Testament hymns.

(i) *1 Timothy iii, 16*

After an introductory sentence: 'Great indeed, we confess, is
the mystery of our religion,' the verse falls into six lines of rich
truth concerning the Person and action of Jesus Christ. By a
series of antithetical couplets in which a second line comple-
ments the thought of the first line, the Gospel message of the
Church's Lord is set forth. It treats of two world orders, the
divine and the human; and shows how Christ has brought together the two spheres by His coming from the glory of the

* See the full study by J. Ysebaert, *Greek Baptismal Terminology.
Its Origin and Early Development* (Nijmegen, 1962).

Father's presence into this world ('revealed in the flesh': cf. John i, 14; Romans viii, 3) and by His lifting up of humanity back again into the divine realm. Thus heaven and earth are joined, and God and man reconciled. His victory is acknowledged in the heavenly regions as the angelic powers confess Him, and upon earth as the Gospel is proclaimed to the nations and accepted in faith.

> 'He was manifested in the flesh,
> Vindicated in the Spirit
> Seen by angels,
> Preached among the nations,
> Believed on in the world,
> Taken up in glory.'

(ii) *Philippians ii, 6–11*

A similar idea of the binding together of the divine realm from which the pre-existent Christ comes and the human domain into which He enters at His birth runs through Philippians ii, 6–11. This is one of the finest Christological portions in the New Testament, and powerfully portrays the drama of Christ's pre-temporal glory with the Father, His abasement and obedience upon earth, even to the death of the Cross, and His exaltation to God's presence and cosmic triumph and lordship which all the spiritual powers confess. There are various suggestions as to how the verses should be arranged.* An analysis into a six-stanza hymn or a three-verse hymn are some widely accepted proposals. It is equally possible that in its original form the Philippians psalm consisted of a series of couplets and belongs to an early tribute to Christ's divine Person. Paul incorporated it into his letter and drew out the important teaching by the insertion of certain interpreting words and phrases. The pre-Pauline verses, set in antiphonal form, may well have read:

> 'He, although He was in the divine Form,
> Did not think equality with God a thing to be grasped;
>
> But surrendered His rank
> And took the role of a servant;

* Reference may be made to the author's contribution, 'The Form-analysis of Philippians ii, 5–11' in *Studia Evangelica II/III* (ed. F. L. Cross: Berlin, 1964), pp. 611–620, and to his forthcoming book on Philippians ii in recent study.

Becoming like the rest of mankind,
And appearing in a human role;

He humbled Himself,
In an obedience that went so far as to die.

For this, God raised Him to the highest honour,
And conferred upon Him the highest rank of all;

That, at Jesus' name every knee should bow,
And every tongue should own that "Jesus Christ is Lord".'

(iii) *Colossians i, 15–20*

As early as 1913 the German scholar, E. Norden,* had
arranged these verses into a hymnic form and detected certain
liturgical traits. His analysis produced the following:

Strophe A

'Who is the image of the unseen God, the first-born of all
    creation
For in Him were created all things in heaven and on earth
Seen and unseen
Whether Thrones or Dominions
Or Powers or Rulers
All things through Him and to Him have been created
And He Himself is before all things,
And all things in Him cohere,
And He Himself is the head of the body, the Church.

Strophe B

Who is the beginning, the first-born from the dead,
That He might become in all things Himself pre-eminent;
 For in Him willed all the Fullness to dwell
And through Him to reconcile all things to Him
Making peace by the blood of His cross,
Through Him, whether those on earth
Or those in heaven.'

It is apparent from this division that the two stanzas cover

† E. Norden, *Agnostos Theos* (Stuttgart, 1913, reprint 1956), p. 252.
Full details of the recent debate on Colossians i, 15–20 will be found in
the author's article in the *Evangelical Quarterly* xxxvi, 1964, pp. 195 ff.

two subjects: Christ and creation (verses 15–18a) and Christ and the Church (verses 18b–20). Moreover, the two parts are comparable in a number of ways and certain stylistic peculiarities are present which cannot be there by chance. For example, we may note the repetition of words and phrases in the two halves, and in some cases the words are repeated in exactly the same position in each stanza. A. M. Hunter* has observed that three pairs of lines are precisely correspondent in the two parts of the hymn. The vocabulary also is unusual and the whole 'betrays the hand of an exacting composer' who penned this noble tribute to exhibit the primacy of Christ in the twin realms of Creation and Redemption. He is portrayed as Lord of the universe and Redeemer of the Church – and Paul uses what appears to be an already existing hymn in order to refute the false doctrines of an incipient Gnosticism which denied the Lord's supremacy and uniqueness as Mediator between God and man. This is not the last time in Christian history when God's people have been kept from error and from lapsing into heresy because they have been recalled to the robust teaching of the traditional hymns of the faith.

(iv) *Hebrews i, 3*

As a final example of what may be adduced as New Testament odes to Christ, we may cite Hebrews i, 3:

> Who reflects the glory of God
> And bears the very stamp of His nature,
> Upholding all things by the word of His power:
> When He had made purification for sins,
> He sat down at the right hand of the majesty on high.'

Again the tell-tale marks of style are evident, such as the use of the relative pronoun ('Who') and participles 'being, upholding, had purged' in A.V.) and the elevated, ceremonial style on which Norden writes: 'It is instructive to notice how this style is the best among New Testament authors.'† The vocabulary too is rare and there is a splendid climax in the sonorous ending of verse 3. By the threefold test of theological content, stylistic construction and unusual vocabulary we may confidently assess this verse to be a Christ-hymn.

It is just as important to notice that these hymns to Christ

* A. M. Hunter, *Paul and his Predecessors* (London, 1961), p. 125
† Norden, op. cit. p. 386.

have a common pattern of thought which makes their presence
in the New Testament canon of the highest value.* They are
related to the Person and mission of Christ Jesus and tell how
He existed in the pre-existent glory of His Father and was the
Agent in creation. He became Man and accomplished redemption for the world through His suffering and death. At length
He is exalted and enthroned and receives from God in a
solemn acclamation the supreme name. This celestial enthrone-
ment as Lord of the universe and all the cosmic spheres which
were thought by first century man to control his destiny by the
stars is acknowledged by all in heaven, on earth and in the
realm of evil spirits. Thus the cosmic dominion of the Church's
Lord is hailed as the answer to the deep need of the human
beings who are held in the iron grip of 'Fate' and whose nerve
has failed. If there is one motif which pervades the New Testament hymns it is this ringing assurance that Christ is victor
over all man's enemies, and is rightly worshipped as the Image
of the God who is over all.

In the second century, the Roman historian Pliny tells of
Christians in Bithynia who sang a hymn to Christ as to God.†
That practice, we may believe, goes back to the New Testament
Church.

* To the passages above may be added: John i, 1–14; 1 Peter i, 18–21;
ii, 21–25; iii, 18–22; and parts of the Revelation which contain distinctively Christian adoration (e.g., v. 9 f.; 12; xii, 10–12; xix, 1 ff.)

† On Pliny's witness to *carmen Christo*, see the writer's study under
that title in *Vox Evangelica* iii (London, 1964), pp. 51–57.

5

'The Pattern of Sound Words' – Early Creeds and Confessions of Faith

The first part of 1 Timothy iii, 16 runs: 'Great indeed, we confess, is the mystery of our religion' (R.S.V.). The Apostle then proceeds to quote the hymn in which the mystery of the Gospel is enshrined – a wonderful truth about the Person and place of Jesus Christ, formerly kept secret but now fully revealed by God – and, in this way, to trace the career of the Church's Lord from His pre-existence, through His incarnate life upon earth, His resurrection and ascension, to His final glory in the Father's presence.

But this specimen of Christian hymnody is much more than a canticle, composed to fill a place in services of worship: the hymn of 1 Timothy iii, 16 is a clear instance of an early confession of faith by which the Church gave expression to the fundamental facts and truths of the Gospel. The first words which are quoted above tell us this explicitly: 'Great indeed, we confess . . .' At this point hymns and creeds meet and overlap.

It is not a simple business to separate the two types of early Christian literature. Following the conclusions at this point of R. Bultmann,* we may say that the first confessions of faith tended to be expressed in short, simple sentences like 'Jesus is the Christ', or 'Jesus Christ is Lord', whereas the hymns represent a longer statement of the Person and work of Christ (as in Philippians ii, 6–11; Colossians i, 15–20) and thus it became possible to split up the hymns into stanzas and sections. But the distinction is not very important. The Church has always delighted to sing its deepest convictions, as in the famous *Te*

* R. Bultmann, art. 'Bekenntnis- und Liedfragmente im ersten Petrusbrief', in *Coniectanea Neotestamentica*, xi, 1947, p. 9.

Deum; and has formulated its most enduring theology in such a way that the common people can easily assimilate the truth as they lift up their hearts and minds to God in anthems of praise and confessions. The great hymns of the Reformation are a monumental witness to this fact; and a Christian leader of the modern Church has said: 'I don't mind who writes the theological books, so long as I can write the hymns!'

The Church as a Believing, Preaching and Confessing Community

We turn to consider what evidence there is in the New Testament Scripture of other credal and confessional forms. It is clear that a full-scale creed in the sense that Dr. J. N. D. Kelly defines it:* 'A fixed formula summarizing the essential articles of (the Christian) religion and enjoying the sanction of ecclesiastical authority' is not found in the pages of the New Testament. But (as Dr. Kelly goes on to show) that is not to imply that the New Testament Church was unconcerned about the doctrinal significance of the message which was believed and proclaimed. Far from it. The Church which greets us in the pages of the New Testament is already a believing, preaching and confessing community of men and women; and this fact implies the existence and influence of a body of authoritative doctrine (although in an embryonic form in certain matters, such as the belief in the Trinity) which was the given and shared possession of those who formed the nascent Christian communities in the world of the Roman Empire. What Paul declared about the Resurrection must have been true about the main tenets of the faith which were cherished and proclaimed: 'Whether then it be I or they (i.e. the other Apostles), so we preach, and so ye believed' (1 Corinthians xv, 11). Only on the assumption of a corpus of doctrine which was accepted as authoritative and binding can we explain the Christian consciousness of the Church's being a distinct entity in the world over against the Jews and Gentiles (1 Corinthians x, 32); and the Church's missionary zeal in proclaiming the Gospel which was *not* offered as a tentative suggestion to be entertained along with other attractive possibilities but as God's unique truth, without rival or peer, and demanding a full and unreserved commitment (see Galatians i, 8, 9; 1 Corinthians xv, 1; 1 Thessalonians ii, 13. The reason for the imperious call of the

* J. N. D. Kelly, *Early Christian Creeds* (London, 1950), p. 1.

Gospel which will brook no rivalry is given in Acts iv, 12 and 2 Corinthians xi, 4: There is only one Saviour and Lord).

Furthermore, only on the ground of the possession of a clearly defined body of Gospel truth can we account for the believers' organizing themselves into communities with a definite cultus (that is, a practised religious devotion which draws men into a society of worshippers or devotees), a standard of belief (2 Corinthians ix, 13; Philippians i, 27) and a precise membership from which defaulters and heretics could be, and in fact were actually, excommunicated (see the examples in 1 Corinthians v, 3–5; 1 Timothy i, 19, 20; 2 John 9, 10) and in which disciplinary measures were exercised (2 Corinthians ii, 5–11). If the early Church had been a society of free-thinkers in which every one was at liberty to believe what he thought acceptable and to live as he pleased, with no guiding lines of doctrine and ethical behaviour patterns, the New Testament Letters would be far different from what we know them. 'The truth of the Gospel' was clearly a doctrinal standard to be jealously preserved (see Galatians ii, 14) and the 'law of Christ' (Galatians vi, 2; 1 Corinthians ix, 21) was a moral directive to be honoured and obeyed.

So far we have discussed the ways in which the New Testament Church shows signs of possessing and using a series of rudimentary creeds and confessions. Now we must examine the evidence to see whether these forms may be located and note the circumstances in which they arose.

I. *The Church's Preaching and Teaching*

In New Testament times, a corpus of distinctive doctrine was held as a sacred deposit from God. The references to such a web of saving truth are set forth with a fulness of description and variety of details, although the evidence must not be pressed to suggest that there was anything approaching the later creeds which are couched in a style and language different from the New Testament. The following places will show how many terms were used by the early Christians:

'The apostles' teaching' (Acts ii, 42).
'The word of life' (Philippians ii, 16).
'The standard of teaching' (Romans vi. 17, R.S.V.).
'The words of faith and good doctrine' (1 Timothy iv, 6).
'The pattern of sound words' (2 Timothy i, 13).
'Sound teaching' (2 Timothy iv, 3; Titus i, 9).

Then there are considerable allusions to 'the faith' (Philippians i, 27; Ephesians iv, 5; Colossians ii, 6, 7; 1 Timothy vi, 20, 21); 'the truth' (Colossians i, 5; 2 Thessalonians ii, 13; 2 Timothy ii, 18, 25; iv, 4); 'the apostolic traditions' (1 Corinthians xi, 2; xv, 1 ff.; Galatians i, 9; Colossians ii, 6; 1 Thessalonians iv, 1; 2 Thessalonians ii, 15); and 'the Gospel' (Romans ii, 16; xvi, 25; 1 Corinthians xv, 1 ff.; Philippians i, 7, 27).

Of this doctrinal formulation the following things are said. First of all, it is to be held fast, especially in time of doubt and when the tendency to apostasy and denial of the faith is marked. Thus it is not surprising that the call to stand fast in the faith and to hold firm to its teaching sounds through the Epistle to the Hebrews, as that letter was addressed to a community of Christians as a 'word of exhortation' (Hebrews xiii, 22) fitted for a group which was in danger of relapsing into their pre-Christian ways (see in the letter, iii, 6, 13; iv, 14; x, 23). The same background of Christians who were faced with the menace of false ideas or heretical tendencies is present in such verses as Jude 3 and 1 John ii, 18–23, while certain expressions of the apostolic faith were designed specifically to refute false doctrines which were raising their head. At Corinth Paul has to deal with a denial of the Resurrection (1 Corinthians xv, 3–5, 12, 35, 36); and in the later Church in Asia Minor an erroneous teaching known as Docetism cast doubt upon the reality of the Lord's incarnation 'in the flesh' and thought only of an 'appearance' in human form. The Apostle John met this subtle heresy with an insistence upon a real incarnation and a veritable humanity which Christ assumed (see 1 John iv, 2, 3; 2 John 7); and did so in a language which has a credal ring about it.

Then, the deposit of the faith is to be cherished and handed on to the succeeding generation of believers (2 Timothy ii, 2), as the apostolic writers themselves had received it from their predecessors in the faith and ultimately from the Lord Himself (1 Corinthians xi, 23 and probably Galatians iv, 14). Oscar Cullmann's discussion* of the way in which the phrase 'from the Lord' (in the Corinthians passage above) is especially important, for he shows how the phrase refers back to 'Christ as the One who stands, not only at the beginning, but also

* O. Cullmann, art. 'KYRIOS as designation for the Oral Tradition concerning Jesus', *Scottish Journal of Theology* iii, 2, 1950, pp. 180–97; and the same author's *The Early Church* (London, E.T., 1956), pp. 59–75.

behind the transmission of the tradition, that is, the One who is at work *in* it. "From the Lord" can mean a direct receiving from the Lord, without it being necessary to think of a vision or of excluding middle-men through whom the Lord imparts the paradosis (tradition) . . . The Apostles are these middle-men . . . and their reality as Apostles lies in their being bearers of direct revelation.'

That St. Paul saw himself as the receiver of an authoritative tradition concerning the Lord's Supper is clear from the terms he uses; and that he understood it as his solemn duty to trans-mit this sacred truth to others is equally evident from the same language. The verbs he employs, 'I received . . . I delivered unto you' are the equivalent to some Rabbinic expressions for the receiving and transmitting of a piece of authoritative teach-ing, and it is important to recall that the former term implies 'the direct reception of specific words'.* The general idea is not the chief concern; it is the precise wording that counts (cf. 1 Corinthians xv, 2 which reads literally, 'in what word I preached the gospel to you') and it is this tradition of 'holy words' which forms a continuous link between the Apostolic age and the succeeding generations of those who came after the Apostles.† The Pauline word in 2 Timothy ii, 2 illustrates the connexion: 'what you have heard from me before many witnesses (cf. 1 Timothy vi, 12) entrust to faithful men who will be able to teach others also' (R.S.V.), as does also the statement in the first Epistle of Clement (*c* A.D. 100), chapter xliv which speaks of 'other eminent men' and 'other approved men' who were appointed to succeed the ministry of the Apostles and their associates.

In the third place, the body of doctrine is referred to in certain contexts as material that is to be utilized in the public proclamation of the Christian message (e.g., Philippians ii, 16; 2 Timothy ii, 15). The most celebrated credal passage which contains the crystallization of Apostolic teaching on the basic elements of the Gospel is 1 Corinthians xv, 3–5. To this we may turn.

We notice immediately the tell-tale marks in this passage

* W. D. Davies, *Paul and Rabbinic Judaism* (London, 1955), p. 249.

† See the important discussion of Birger Gerhardsson, *Memory and Manuscript* (Uppsala, 1961), Part 2: 'The Delivery of the Gospel Tradi-tion in Early Christianity,' with an assessment by W. D. Davies, printed as Appendix xv to the latter's book, *The Setting of the Sermon on the Mount* (Cambridge, 1964).

which stamp it as a credal formulary.* The four-fold 'that' introduces each member of the creed (in verses 3, 4, 5). The vocabulary is unusual, containing some rare terms and expressions which Paul never employs again. The preface to the section informs us that Paul 'received' what follows in his next sentences as part of the instruction, no doubt, he had known in the early days of his discipleship, possibly through his contacts with the Church at Jerusalem and Antioch and Damascus. And now in turn, he transmits (using the same technical expressions as in 1 Corinthians xi, 23) to the Corinthian Church what he has received as a sacred tradition. The matter of the suggested background of this passage and its pre-Pauline and credal origin is clinched by verse 11 of the chapter, where Paul remarks that he has stated what was the common proclamation of the Apostles: 'Whether then it was I or they, so we preach and so you believed.'

Recent studies have shown the importance of this pre-Pauline passage.† There has been a reaction against the view that these verses reproduce a summary of Christian belief held by the Greek-speaking Churches which Paul learned of when he came into touch with these communities (notably at Antioch: see Acts xiii, 1). There are certain indications in the text itself that 1 Corinthians xv, 3 ff. is a translation into Greek of a piece of Aramaic. The most obvious points are that Peter's name is given in its Semitic form as Cephas, and that there is a double reference to the Old Testament Scriptures. Professor Jeremias argues,‡ with some cogency, that these verses arose in a Jewish-Christian *milieu*; and more recently still a Scandinavian scholar§ has submitted that this piece of Christian creed emanated from the earliest Palestinian Church. It represents, he says, 'a logos (i.e. statement of belief) fixed by the college of Apostles in Jerusalem' and finds in this fact a confirmation of the way in which Paul expressed his respect for Jerusalem as the city of God in the last days, from which the word of the Lord would proceed to the nations in fulfilment of the prophetic hope of the Old Testament (Isaiah ii, 2–4). If this argu-

* For the details, see J. Jeremias, *The Eucharistic Words of Jesus* (Oxford, E.T., 1955), pp. 129 f.

† The most comprehensive study is that of E. Lichtenstein, art. 'Die älteste christliche Glaubensformel,' *Zeitsch. f. Kirchengeschichte*, lxiii, 1950, pp. 4–74. See too B. Gerhardsson, op. cit., pp. 295 ff. and A. M. Hunter, *Paul and his Predecessors* [London,] 1961), pp. 117 f.

‡ Jeremias, op. cit., p. 130.

§ B. Gerhardsson, op. cit., p. 297.

ment is sound, it is clear that the passage belongs to the very earliest days of the Church and is, as E. Meyer phrased it, 'the oldest document of the Christian Church in existence'.* It goes back to the teaching of the Hebrew-Christian fellowship shortly after the death of Christ, and may well embody the fruit of the post-Resurrection instruction and reflection contained in Luke xxiv, 25–27, 44–47. Within a few years of the redeeming events of the Cross and the Empty Grave, the followers of the Lord were confessing that:

> Christ died for our sins
>   according to the Scriptures.
> He was buried:
> He was raised on the third day
>   according to the Scriptures.
> He appeared to Cephas,
> then to the Twelve.

II. The Church's Worship

Dr. Vernon H. Neufeld has subjected all the New Testament confessions of faith to a close inspection,† and has concluded that the earliest form of Christian witness may be taken back into the period of the Gospel record and to the disciples' utterance, 'Jesus is the Christ' (Mark viii, 29). The question of Jesus' messiahship was a live issue in the period covered by the Acts of the Apostles and the Christian mission to the Jews of the Dispersion; and it is not surprising that the confession 'Jesus is the Messiah' is found as a major theme in the early parts of the New Testament (e.g., Acts ix, 22). From the fact that this exact confession runs through the Gospel of John, Neufeld argues that this Gospel is to be placed in the early stages of the growth of the New Testament literature. The title 'Christ' features in the call of Peter in Acts ii, 38 which in turn is concerned with a baptismal scene.

As the Church moved out into a Gentile environment the debate concerning Messiahship became an irrelevant issue; and it is therefore quite to be expected that in Paul's dealings with the Gentile Churches of the Roman Empire the Messianic status of Jesus will be of a secondary concern. This is precisely what we find in the Apostle's language. 'In the Epistles Paul

* E. Meyer, *Ursprung und Anfänge des Christentums* III (Berlin, 1923), p. 210.
† V. H. Neufeld, *The Earliest Christian Confessions* (Leiden, 1963).

never says "Jesus is the Christ" . . . He never seems to have
laid much stress on teaching the Gentiles the meaning of the
name.'* The appropriate appellation is Lord; and this, for him,
is the vital thing. 'If you confess with your lips that Jesus is
Lord . . . you will be saved' (Romans x, 9). 'For we preach not
ourselves but Christ Jesus as Lord' (2 Corinthians iv, 5). 'No
one can say "Jesus is Lord" except by the Holy Spirit' (1
Corinthians xii, 3).

The confession 'Jesus Christ is Lord' may be placed in the
setting of the Church's worshipping life. We have just seen that
it is a fitting formula by which the new convert testified to his
faith in Christ; and we glean from the record in the Acts of the
Apostles that conversion and baptism were regarded as the
inside and outside of the same experience. Acts ii, 37, 38 speaks
of both the inquiry, 'What shall we do?' and the Apostle's
directive, 'Repent, and be baptized every one of you in the
name of Jesus Christ.' Here is a scene when the initial confession of the lordship of Christ (see Acts ii, 36: 'God hath
made him both Lord and Christ') was most appropriate and
in order. There are two other places where the same initial
answer to the Gospel's call was followed immediately by the
submission to the baptismal rite: Acts viii, 35–38, and Acts
xvi, 33.

The first passage is of considerable interest, mainly because
the important Western textual tradition preserves the actual
terms in which the confession was made. At verse 36, there are
the words: 'and Philip said to him, If thou believest with all
thine heart, it is permitted (to you to be baptized): and he
answered and said, I believe that Jesus Christ is the Son of
God.' Then follows the record of the eunuch's baptism at the
hands of Philip the evangelist. The interest here is that quite
possibly this addition represents the earliest form of a baptismal creed. At the baptism of converts some inquiry would be
made as to faith in Christ, and a simple confession and attestation of belief and allegiance to Him called for. The dialogue
between the evangelist and the newly-awakened believer in
Acts viii mirrors what must have happened often before the
administration of the ordinance; and the later history of baptismal practice confirms this piece of evidence.

* N. A. Dahl, art. 'Die Messianität Jesu bei Paulus' in *Studia Paulina*
(ed. J. N. Sevenster and W. C. van Unnik: Haarlem, 1953), p. 94,
quoted by A. M. Hunter, *Interpreting Paul's Gospel* (London, 1954), p.
61.

The three best-known baptismal interrogations are preserved in the writings of Justin Martyr (*c.* A.D. 100–165); Irenaeus (*c.* A.D. 130–200)* and Hippolytus of Rome (*c.* A.D. 215). The fullest form is contained in the last-named which describes a three-fold immersion and a three-fold profession of faith, corresponding to the three Persons of the Trinity. The questions and responses run:†

Dost thou believe in God the Father Almighty?
I believe.

Dost thou believe in Christ Jesus, the Son of God,
Who was born of the Holy Spirit and the Virgin Mary,
Who was crucified in the days of Pontius Pilate,
And died (*and was buried*)
And rose the third day living from the dead
And ascended into the heavens,
And sat down at the right hand of the Father,
And will come to judge the living and the dead?
I believe.

Dost thou believe in (*the*) Holy Spirit in the Holy Church,
And the resurrection of the flesh?
I believe.

Acts xvi, 31–33 is a cameo of the conversion of the Philippian jailer and his household, with the result that, having believed in God with all his household and family, he was baptized in response to the Apostle's call: 'Put your trust in the Lord Jesus (or, in Jesus as Lord), and you will be saved, you and your household.'

Ephesians v, 25, 26 may be mentioned here, following C. A. Anderson Scott's translation of the Pauline words: ‡ 'Christ loved the church, and gave himself up for her, that he might consecrate her after cleansing in the water-bath (of baptism) together with the Formula'; and by the formula (literally, 'saying') Paul evidently means the public acknowledgement by the persons to be baptized of Jesus as Lord.

In another place (Philippians ii, 11) Paul quotes the

* See J. N. D. Kelly, op. cit., pp. 73, 77; and K. Runia, *I Believe in God . . .* (London, 1963), p. 20 f.

† The translation is that by G. Dix, *The Apostolic Tradition of St. Hippolytus of Rome* (London, 1937), pp. 36 f.

‡ C. A. A. Scott, *Christianity according to St. Paul* (Cambridge, 1932), p. 119.

confessional acclamation: 'Jesus Christ is Lord.' As was noted before, this cry comes as the climax of the hymnic adoration of the cosmic Christ as all creatures throughout the universe bow down and submit to His dominion. A recent study of the passage by the Scandinavian scholar J. Jervell* has sought to place this hymn and its closing acclamation in a baptismal context. The cogency of this ingenious argument depends upon the acceptance of certain assumptions which the author makes. These are (i) that the confession of Christ's lordship is primarily concerned with the submission of the evil spirit-forces which assent to His victory over them and their consequent defeat; (ii) that the mention of the 'name' links up with other references to the calling of Christ's name over the convert in baptism; and (iii) that the term 'form' in Philippians ii, 6 is to be equated in meaning with 'image'. We may therefore bring into the discussion those texts in which the image of Christ is said to be formed and seen in the believer (especially Philippians iii, 10, 21; 2 Corinthians iii, 18; Romans viii, 29; Galatians iv, 19). Jervell then proceeds to argue that it was by union with Christ in the sacrament of baptism that the image of Christ began to take shape within the Christian (as in Romans vi, 3–5; Galatians v, 24; Colossians ii, 12).

The final line of reasoning runs as follows. The confession of Jesus Christ as Lord by the convert may well have betokened for him the passing from the domain of the spirit-powers by which his old life was controlled (cf. Galatians iv, 3–9; 1 Corinthians xii, 2) into the liberty and joy of the Gospel (see Romans viii, 15, 21, 38 f.; Galatians v, 1 ff.; Colossians i, 12 f.; ii, 8–15). The old life, like the old nature, was put away; and the new convert put on Christ, the new man in whose image he was renewed and reborn (Ephesians iv, 22–24; Colossians iii, 9–12). By submitting to the act of baptism into Christ he is called to live out the life of his Lord as he becomes conformed to that image. Thus Christ 'takes shape' (Galatians iv, 19) in him from the very moment of conversion-baptism; and the hymn which powerfully sets the person of Christ as the Image of God and His victory and exaltation may well have been sung at the service of baptism when the Church is reminded of the need to live out the life of that Lord who is the conqueror of all the foes which menaced first century man and held him in bondage to fear and his lower nature.

* J. Jervell, *Imago Dei: Gen. 1. 26 f. im Spätjudentum, in der Gnosis und in den paulinischen Briefen* (Göttingen, 1960), pp. 206–209.

If there is any truth in this attempt to place the Philippians ii hymn in such a setting, it would provide yet one more endorsement of the general view that the affirmation 'Jesus Christ is Lord' belongs to the cultic life of the early Christians as they engaged in their worship of the sovereign Master of their lives and of the universe.

III. *The Church's Witness Against Paganism*

The early Church was called to live its life and maintain its testimony in tumultuous times. As early as the first preaching in Acts and the Pauline missionary tours, the fires of persecution are seen clearly in all their intensity; and we read that Christians are being haled before Jewish authorities and Roman officials, and required to attest their allegiance to Jesus Christ. It is not unexpected, therefore, that the Christian confessions should have been shaped by this process. In time of conflict and duress the distinctive and dearly-cherished forms of the faith are crystallized and moulded.

The prototype of these statements of belief goes back to the Lord's own *credo* before the Sanhedrin at His trial recorded in Mark xiv, 61, 62 and xv, 2. The Apostle makes allusion to this in reminding Timothy of 'Christ Jesus, who before Pontius Pilate witnessed a good confession', in a passage which reproduces 'the substance of a primitive baptismal creed'.* The point at issue is the need to stand firm in the face of opposition even as the Lord Jesus, when arraigned before His earthly judges, both Jewish and Roman, bore witness to a 'noble confession'. The call to such a confession had already been hinted in Jesus' own words in Matthew x, 32, 33.

The arraignment of Christians before Jewish tribunals was chiefly of an incidental character, and the punishment they received was occasioned largely by hysterical outbursts of indignation and wrath. Such a circumstance would hardly leave room for a formal declaration of belief. But as the Church came into collision with the Roman authorities, the questions which the Romans asked were such as to elicit careful statements of the faith.

Oscar Cullmann† has set forth the theory that the formula-

* J. N. D. Kelly, *The Pastoral Epistles* (London, 1963), p. 143.
† O. Cullmann, *The Earliest Christian Confessions* (London, E.T., 1949), pp. 28 ff.

tion of early creeds was controlled partly by the apologetic needs of the Church as it faced the hostile and pagan world. When haled before the Roman magistrate, and required to make some attestation of supreme loyalty to Christ, the Christians confessed, 'Jesus Christ is Lord', not Caesar. This is the historical background of Acts xvii, 5–10, xviii, 12–17.

Cullmann wishes to suggest the same setting for 1 Corinthians xii, 3. The true Christians, inspired by the Spirit, whose help is promised (Matthew x, 19, 20), will never curse Christ (and say, 'Jesus is anathema'), but will attest 'Jesus is Lord', as Polycarp and the later martyrs did. The *Martyrdom of Polycarp*, written as an eye-witness account of the bishop of Smyrna in the early years of the second century, is a moving document of the aged man's refusal to swear allegiance to Caesar by saying 'Lord Caesar' (*Mart. Pol.* viii, 2) and thereby denying his Lord Christ (*Mart. Pol.* ix, 3).

While the evidence from Polycarp's martyrdom looks to be parallel with the wording of 1 Corinthians xii, 3, it is doubtful if Cullmann's suggestion can be sustained, for there is no hint of persecution in 1 Corinthians. It is more likely that the background is the readmission of apostate Christians to the synagogue, when the declaration required would be 'Jesus is accursed' (in the sense of Deuteronomy xxi, 23) – and therefore no true Messiah – in reversal of the orthodox confession, 'Jesus is Lord'. The point, however, which Cullmann's view makes is still a valid one, namely, that the early Christians in their struggle against both Jews and Gentiles, expressed the nub and gist of what distinguished them by simple formulas of confessions. And in the later Church this led to the class of persons known as 'confessors' who were called upon to attest their allegiance to Christ as well as the 'martyrs' who sealed that testimony with their blood.

The Range of the Early Creeds

The confessions of the New Testament extend from the simple 'Jesus is Lord' to the detailed summaries of 1 Corinthians xv, 3–5; Romans i, 3, 4; iv, 24, 25, viii, 34; Philippians ii, 6–11; 1 Timothy iii, 16 and 1 Peter iii, 18–22. As confessions of Christ, they comprehend the various aspects of His Person (both pre-existent and incarnate); His mission (His death, burial, descent into the underworld of Hades); and His victory and exalted status and role as Intercessor and Lord of all.

There are also binitarian creeds* which unite the Father and the Son (1 Corinthians viii, 6; 1 Timothy ii, 5 f.). Nor should we overlook the implicit Trinitarian fragments such as Matthew xxviii, 19; 2 Corinthians i, 21 f.; xiii, 14; 1 Corinthians vi, 11; xii, 4 f. There are also those verses which are shaped in a triadic scheme, which set out the 'division of work' of the Trinity – the Father who sends, the Son who is sent, and the Spirit who applies the work of salvation (see Galatians iii, 11–14; iv, 4 f.; 1 Peter i, 2; Hebrews x, 29). Here are the raw materials of the later fully developed Trinitarian creeds which bid us praise:

> Glory to the Father,
> Glory to the Son.
> And to Thee, blest Spirit,
> While all ages run.

* See Runia, op. cit., pp. 18 ff.

6

The Ministry of the Word

In an earlier chapter we considered the two religious institutions which meant so much to the Judaism of the first decades of our Christian era – the Temple in Jerusalem, and the network of synagogues which were found in Palestine and through the Dispersion of the Jewish people in the Roman Empire. Of these two institutions, the Temple worship was the more impressive and splendid, with its ceremonial and functionaries. But the influence of the synagogue on Christian worship was more permanent and deep. W. D. Maxwell suggests two reasons for this.*

The first is that the great majority of Jews scattered throughout the Empire had never seen the Temple, while naturally for the Gentiles who became Christians it meant little as an imposing architectural sight. For Jews living in Palestine, the local synagogue in their town or village was much more real in every sense than the Temple in far-away metropolitan Zion. The second reason is found in the historical circumstance that, forty years after the death of Jesus, the Temple was destroyed and its importance was permanently eclipsed; the synagogues remained.

As we saw in chapter 2, the chief element in the worship practised in the synagogue was the reading and exposition of the Law. The Law was read, first in the original Hebrew and then in Aramaic paraphrases, known as Targums, followed in turn by a homily. This is the centre of gravity of the synagogue's service, with the blessings and prayers gathered round it. We are now to see how this pattern was carried over into Christian assemblies, and the place which the early believers gave to the ministry of the Word.

References to the Jewish pattern are made in Luke iv, 16–27 and Acts xiii, 14 ff. In both cases there is the customary reading from the Scriptures, followed by an explanation or 'word of

* W. D. Maxwell, op. cit., p. 2.

exhortation' (Acts xiii, 15). At Nazareth, Jesus was both the reader of the 'Lesson for the day' in Isaiah lxi, 1 f. and the 'preacher' who proceeded to interpret and apply to the hearers the passage which He had just read out. For Paul the invitation to give this 'word' was just the opportunity he sought in his policy to evangelize the Jews 'first' (see Acts xiii, 46; Romans i, 16; ix, 1–5). He proclaimed Christ to the men of Abraham's stock as the fulfilment of the Law and the Prophets, and the Saviour of the nation of Israel (Acts xiii, 23). It cannot be fortuitous that this message is precisely the import of Jesus' own declaration at Nazareth, when after the reading of the Prophetic lesson, known as the *Haphtarah*, He immediately applied the fulfilment of prophecy to Himself: 'Today is this scripture fulfilled in your hearing.'

The persuasiveness of Paul's ministry is evidenced in a number of ways – some of his hearers were won over (Acts xiii, 42, 43), others were stirred up to wrath and opposition (Acts xiii, 44 ff.). It seems that the one thing which was impossible as an outcome of Paul's synagogue ministry was indifference and unconcern. It was only at Athens where Paul met the Greeks on ground which was unfamiliar to him that his message was greeted with a cynical disdain (Acts xvii, 18, 32).

The same outcome of his ministry in the synagogue followed at Iconium (Acts xiv, 1 ff.), while at Thessalonica (Acts xvii, 1 ff.) we read of some consecutive ministry in the Jewish meeting-house there. The Archbishop of York has made the interesting suggestion that verses 2, 3 which speak of Paul's stay for three weeks also give the themes of his preaching on three successive Sabbaths – the first, that the Christ must suffer; the second, that He must rise again; the third, that this Jesus is the Christ of whom the Old Testament prophesies such things.*

At all events, we are assured that the Apostle's ministry was based on the Scriptures, as he sought to demonstrate that the Old Testament speaks of Christ; that it is, as Luther later declared, the crib in which Christ is laid. An even longer ministry in the synagogue was made possible at Ephesus (Acts xix, 8) to be succeeded by a period of Christian instruction in a hired room each day during the hot afternoon hours when most people in Ephesus would be enjoying their siesta. This picture – and how the imagination is stirred to reconstruct the scene of Paul exercising an energetic speaking ministry to an

* F. D. Coggan, *The Ministry of the Word* (London, 1945), p. 103.

eager-faced band of listeners, while the city outside was wrapped in a sleepy silence. The commentators Lake and Cadbury* observe that normally more people would be asleep in Ephesus at 1 p.m. than at 1 in the early morning! – is preserved for us in a secondary reading in Acts xix, 9. The Western text which provides some additional and fascinating side-lights on Paul's career in Acts amplifies the reference to the lecture-room of Tyrannus by including the time-note: 'from the fifth to the tenth hour'. This means that from 11 a.m. to 4 p.m. when the hall was free and the Ephesians slept, Paul and his followers took over the hired premises for the purposes of Bible study!

The Berean Jews are commended not only for the close attention which they gave to what Paul said in their synagogue, but also for the way in which they acted upon his ministry. They 'examined the scriptures daily' to see if the things he said were true (Acts xvii, 11). We may surmise with some confidence as to the result of this Bible-searching, for it is reported that '*therefore* many of them came to believe'.

The examples we have so far considered relate to the Apostle's use of the synagogue as a spring-board for his preaching and Bible-instruction ministry. We must press our inquiry further to see if there is evidence of Scripture reading and exposition in a distinctively Christian setting.

I. *The Public Reading of the Scriptures*

In the minister's manual which we call 1 Timothy, the young pastor is encouraged with the following admonition: 'Devote your attention to the public reading of the scriptures' (iv, 13, N.E.B.). This text forms part of a list of ministerial functions in which the Apostle's coadjutor is to engage as he conducts public Church services. This task of the public reading of the Scriptures is then quite distinct from the private study counselled in 2 Timothy iii, 15–17. But what is said in the latter place about the nature and purpose of the Scripture makes the matter of the public reading of it one of supreme importance. Because the Scripture is 'given by inspiration of God' and consequently 'profitable for instruction, for reproof, for correction, and for training in uprightness', and above all, 'able to

* Lake and Cadbury in *The Beginnings of Christianity*, Vol. IV (London, 1933), p. 239.

make' the hearer 'wise unto salvation through faith which is in Christ Jesus', the place which it holds in the ordering of divine service must always be central and determinative. This is an inheritance we have received, through the early Church, from the worship of Judaism, and which makes the model Christian service (in the expressive Continental phrase) a Word-of-God service.* Our interest in the earlier verse in 1 Timothy is secured by the fact that it is the first historical allusion to the use of the Scriptures in the Church's liturgy, for the reference in 2 Corinthians iii, 14 to the reading of the 'old covenant' and of 'Moses' seems clearly to point to a liturgical reading of the Pentateuch in the synagogue as distinct from a Christian meeting.

In the later Church the evidence is more abundant than this abbreviated notice to Timothy. About the year A.D. 150 Justin Martyr describes a Sunday service in Rome† and tells us how 'the memoirs of the Apostles and the writings of the Prophets are read as long as time permits. Then, when the reader has finished, the President speaks, admonishing and exhorting the people to follow noble teaching and examples.' There are two points of immediate interest in this testimony. First, we are reminded that, as in the Pastoral epistles, the Scripture lection is taken from the Church's Bible, the Old Testament. But by the time when Justin writes, the New Testament has achieved a canonical status and the 'memoirs of the Apostles' are placed alongside the Old Testament as authoritative liturgical documents. The way in which this evolution developed is mentioned below.

Then, the office of 'reader' is hinted at in Justin's description. Dr. Kelly has recently called attention to the importance of this function in the early Church. 'Public reading in the ancient world called for some technical accomplishment, for the words in the codex (or book) were not divided.'‡ It is therefore only to be expected that some educated and trained person in the congregation will come forward and offer his service as official 'lector'. Traces of his activity may be detected in Matthew xxiv, 15; Mark xiii, 14 and Revelation i, 3, while in the following Church era there are many allusions to his important position.§

* Thus in the title of W. Bauer's book, *Der Wortgottesdienst der ältesten Christen* (Tübingen, 1930).
† Justin, *First Apology*, chapter lxvii.
‡ J. N. D. Kelly, *The Pastoral Epistles*, p. 105.
§ See the details supplied by L. E. Elliott-Binns, *The Beginnings of Western Christendom* (London, 1948), p. 324.

Apart from the Pauline reference in 1 Timothy iv, 13 there is little else to build on in the Apostolic age; and some scholars (notably G. Delling)* have denied that the Old Testament was ever read as part of Christian worship in the first century. But there is presumptive evidence that this denial is too cautious. The way in which St. Paul expects his Gentile readers to be acquainted with the Old Testament seems conclusively to show that their services must have included a lectionary reading of the sacred literature of Judaism. For his allusions are not simply to the general drift of the Old Testament story; rather he is concerned with subtle details and undertones.† See, for example, Romans iv, 1–23; ix, 7–9; Galatians iii, 6–9; iv, 21 ff.; 1 Corinthians vi, 16; x, 1 ff.; 2 Corinthians iii, 7–18. He taught them to see in the Gospel the realization of Scripture's original purpose (Romans xv, 4; 1 Corinthians ix, 9), both of encouragement and of warning (1 Corinthians x, 6, 11; Galatians iv, 21; v, 1), as well as the fulfilment of God's ancient promise of revelation and redemption (2 Corinthians i, 20; Galatians iii, 6 ff.).

Above all, Paul insists, the Old Testament is a true 'preparation for the Gospel'. The Scripture (which is almost personified) convicts men of their need (Galatians iii, 22) and drives them to Christ (Galatians iii, 24). It explains the Gospel in advance (Galatians iii, 8) and in retrospect (1 Corinthians xv, 3–5). For these reasons, the Old Testament is to be regarded as 'holy scripture' (Romans i, 2), with an authority which is to be acknowledged and obeyed (2 Timothy iii, 16, 17), even though its story is incomplete and awaits the coming of Christ (2 Corinthians iii, 7–18). On its own and without the interpreting and complementary witness of the New Testament, the Old Testament is a book of unfulfilled prophecies, unexplained ceremonies, and unsatisfied longings.‡ Yet as a witness to Christ and a preparation for His advent and Kingdom, it holds an unrivalled place; and its place and importance in the worship of Christ's people are assured. The Lord's own words recorded in Luke xxiv, 27 have been the guide and incentive to the Christians' study of the Old Testament in both private devotion and public assembly.

* G. Delling, *Worship in the New Testament* (London, E.T., 1962), pp. 92 ff.

† For the Apostle's use of the Old Testament in Romans i–viii, see the detailed analysis by L. C. Allen in an essay under that title in *Vox Evangelica iii* (London, 1964).

‡ This description is borrowed from W. H. Griffith Thomas, *The Principles of Theology* (London, 1945 ed.), p. 136.

We are on surer grounds in our affirmation that early Christian worship included the element of Scripture reading when it comes to the question of the reading of the New Testament documents. Paul expected that his Letters would be read out in the public convocation of the Churches (Colossians iv, 16; 1 Thessalonians v, 27; Philemon 2). And we may compare again the reference to the 'reader' in Revelation i, 3 which the R.S.V. correctly renders: 'Blessed is he who reads aloud the words of the prophecy. . . .' See too at the close of this book: 'I Jesus have sent my angel to you with this testimony for the churches' (xxii, 16).

A recent theory proposes that the ending of 1 Corinthians is a bridge between the reading of the Letter to the gathered Church and an ensuing Communion service. Hans Lietzmann has described the scene as he sees it.* 'We are among the assembled Christians at Corinth (as we read chapter xvi, 20–24). A letter of the apostle is being read aloud – it is drawing to its conclusion – another exhortation to amendment of life, to love and peace and unity. Then the solemn words ring out – verses 20 f. The epistle is concluded and – the Lord's Supper begins'.

Before the close of the New Testament canon,† Paul's Letters were receiving special attention and were being accepted as on a par with 'other scriptures' (2 Peter iii, 15, 16). He had expected them to be accepted as authoritative in his lifetime (e.g., 2 Thessalonians ii, 15; iii, 14) for the Churches to which they were sent. Especially when his authority was controverted, he is insistent that his written word is charged with the Lord's *imprimatur*: 'If any one thinks that he is a prophet, or spiritual, he should acknowledge that what I am writing to you is a command of the Lord' (1 Corinthians xiv, 37, R.S.V.). Gradually his Letters became more widely known and accepted, as they were circulated among the Churches and read out in public gathering. In this way they became the object of study and meditation,‡ although it is an unsolved mystery why some areas of Church life in the second century seem quite

* H. Lietzmann, *Mass and Lord's Supper* (Leiden, E.T., 1953), Fasc. iv, p. 186. See too G. Dix, *The Shape of the Liturgy* (London, 1945), p. 107, n. 7.

† For the complex issues connected with canonicity, see the contribution on this subject by H. Ridderbos to *Revelation and the Bible* (ed. C. F. H. Henry: London, 1959), pp. 189 ff.

‡ The classic study of this matter is that by A. E. Barnett, *Paul becomes a Literary Influence* (Chicago, 1941).

untouched by his influence and ignorant of his writings. Yet
Polycarp is able to write to the Philippians (some time between
110–117) and say of the Pauline Letters: 'from the study of
which you will be able to be built up into the faith'. P. N.
Harrison* renders the first words of this quotation, '*if* ye pore
over them'; and this verb became a favourite expression for the
diligent application of heart and mind to what was read out in
public worship as the Apostolic literature was elevated to the
rank of Scripture.

An interesting vignette of Church life in the later decades of
the second century shows how much valued the Apostle's
writings were. In July A.D. 180 twelve Christians, seven men
and five women, were put to death at Carthage in North Africa.
They came from Scillium and so are known as the Scillitan
martyrs. The account of their trial and sufferings is preserved,
written in the artless simplicity of a non-literary style, but containing the actual words of the dialogue between the Roman
proconsul and the Christian spokesman. When asked by the
former about a certain box in their possession, the martyrs
replied that it contained 'the books (i.e. the Gospels) and the
epistles of Paul the righteous'.

In this illustration and in the testimony of Justin a few
decades earlier, we find mention made of the Gospels. It is
plausible that the motives which led to the composition and
growth of the Four Gospels may be traced to the exigencies of
public worship. Christians had long been familiar with oral
traditions concerning the sayings and deeds of the incarnate
Lord, but as the original disciples (like Mnason, Acts xxi, 16;
see N.E.B.) and eyewitnesses (spoken of in Luke i, 2) were
taken away by death, the need for a permanent record was felt;
and this desire for a more durable record may have been en-
hanced by the awareness that the Lord's return was not
imminent and that more than one generation of Christians must
be provided for. In this way, what had been passed on orally
at the public gatherings for worship on the Lord's day became
arranged into a codified form, and may have been grouped as
a definite lectionary. The compiling of such narratives is suggested in the frontispiece to Luke's Gospel (Luke i, 1), and
many writers are said to have put their hand to this enterprise;
and it is a possible theory which submits that the original testimony to Jesus' life and ministry, given first by eyewitnesses

* P. N. Harrison, *Polycarp's Two Epistles to the Philippians* (Cambridge,
1936) on Polycarp's letter iii. 2. (p. 322).

and ministers of the word, became embodied in the form in which we have it in the canonical Gospels by some process of lectionary usage. Our different Gospels may conceivably be the Gospel lections of the various centres of early Christianity like Rome and Antioch. Thus the memoirs of the Apostles (in Justin's phrase) took their place along with the Apostolic epistles as canonical Scripture, although isolated sayings of the Lord were received as binding in the 'oral' period (see 1 Thessalonians iv, 15; 1 Corinthians xi, 23; vii, 10; ix, 14; Acts xx, 35; 1 Timothy v, 18).

II. *The Church's Preaching*

What can we know about the sermon in New Testament times? The missionary preaching of the Apostles is well reported in the book of the Acts of the Apostles; and from this material scholars have, with some plausibility, reconstructed the New Testament *kerygma* or public proclamation of the Gospel. The places in Acts which are most germane are: ii, 14–39; iii, 12–26; iv, 8–12; x, 36–43, while the sermons at Lystra (iv, 15–17) and Athens (xvii, 22–31) have a style and slant all of their own. In the later section of Acts there are occasional references to the Gospel's content in such public testimony before Roman governors and other dignitaries (thus fulfilling Acts ix, 15) as St. Paul was called upon to bear. For instance, Acts xxvi, 22, 23 contains a summary of the Gospel in miniature, but emphasizing the distinctive notes of the fulfilment of Old Testament prophecy ('what the prophets and Moses said'), the death of the Messiah, His rising from the dead and the mission to the Gentile peoples.

Thanks to the labours and insights of such writers as C. H. Dodd and A. M. Hunter* – the gains of which have been harvested in a recent book by R. H. Mounce under the title, *The Essential Nature of New Testament Preaching*† – we can set down the outstanding themes of the public proclamation of the 'way of salvation' (Acts xvi, 17). The early preachers had certain subjects and motifs to which they returned again and again. These are:

(i) The age of fulfilment has dawned; the Old Testament

* C. H. Dodd, *The Apostolic Preaching and its Developments* (London, 1936: new ed. 1963), chapter 4. A. M. Hunter, *The Unity of the New Testament* (London, 1943)

† R. H. Mounce, *The Essential Nature of New Testament Preaching* (Grand Rapids, 1960).

prophecies have been realized; the hope of Israel is now a present fact (Acts ii, 16; iii, 18, 24; x, 43).

(ii) This fulfilment is shown by the life, death and resurrection of Jesus the Messiah (ii, 30; x, 37 f.; v, 30; x, 39; ii, 24, 32, iii, 15; ii, 33).

(iii) In virtue of His resurrection He is exalted as Lord (ii, 33–36; iii, 13; iv, 11).

(iv). The Holy Spirit's presence in the Church is a token of God's favour toward His people (ii, 44, 17–21; v, 32).

(v) Christ will come again as Judge and Saviour (iii, 20 f.; x, 42; xvii, 31).

(vi) There is an appeal for repentance, an offer of forgiveness and the gift of the Holy Spirit, and an assurance of salvation (ii, 38; iii, 19; x, 43).

It is true that this neat scheme of Apostolic ministry has been challenged.* Some scholars wish to amend the list of items, whether by addition or by omission. In the first category will be placed the suggestion of T. F. Glasson that the early preaching included the note of *witness* – a frequently found word in the speeches in Acts. Dr. Mounce queries whether the second Advent of Christ formed a major item in the *public* preaching in view of the paucity of allusion to this doctrine. Other scholars have wondered whether this stereotyped and formal analysis does justice to the element of spontaneity and freedom which characterized the early preaching in its pristine quality of freshness and exuberance. Thus one critic of C. H. Dodd's book writes: 'I confess that Dodd's *kerygma* leaves me with a feeling of having been robbed of the fulness of Christ in the interests of a unified formula, although at the same time I would accept his conclusions.'†

The point is well taken, and any reconstruction of the primitive preaching should avoid the impression that the items can be tabulated and dissected in a formal way. The message of the Apostles related to the miraculous inbreaking of God into human life in the Person and work of His Son, the Messiah of Israel's hope and the Saviour of men. Such news could not be captured within the compass of a neat, standardized formula. The period of stylization and formulation came later. The preaching in Acts carries the overtone of warmth and enthusi-

* References are given in Mounce, op. cit., pp. 60 ff.

† P. Davies, art. 'Unity and Variety in the New Testament', *Interpretation* v, 1951, p. 182.

asm as the utterances of men who could be mistaken for drunken (Acts ii, 13, 15).

None the less, with this caveat, it is possible to detect certain specific themes on which the first preachers concentrated both their interest and their hearers' attention. These were the death of Jesus the Christ – an event which both fulfilled Old Testament anticipations and involved human responsibility, yet all in the divine purpose of grace. These notes are sounded in Acts iii, 18; iii, 13, 14 and ii, 23. But when men had done their worst and rejected God's gift by nailing Him to a tree (v, 30; x, 39), God stepped in and reversed the verdict by raising the Crucified from the dead. The Resurrection is by common consent the decisive element in the *kerygma* and its note runs through the early chapters of Acts like a haunting refrain: 'This Jesus hath God raised up, whereof we all are witnesses.' He was raised, and He was seen by us, the Apostles, are the twin aspects of this triumphant declaration (ii, 32; iii, 15; iv, 20; v, 32; x, 41). Moreover, God has exalted His Son as the logical sequel to the Resurrection, a fact attested by prophecy and by the present experience of the Holy Spirit who is given to believers as the gift of the ascended Lord.

On the basis of these facts – whether of fulfilled prophecy or historical detail in the ministry of Jesus in Galilee and Jerusalem or the Apostles' own experience of the living Christ and the Spirit's presence with them – the conclusion is drawn. God has made Him both Lord and Christ (Acts ii, 36), two titles which sum up all the names which these chapters give to Him.*

But the preaching was not a 'dispassionate recital of historical facts – a sort of nondescript presentation of certain truths, interesting enough, but morally neutral'.† The facts were meant to become factors in the lives of the auditors; hence the summons to repentance and revaluation, and the offer of pardon and a place in that new Age which God had inaugurated by the coming of His Son. Peter's closing words in his Pentecostal sermon are couched in the strong language of the imperative: 'Repent, and be baptized . . . save yourselves from this crooked generation.' Yet this is but the negative side. The hearers were to be saved *into* the fellowship of the Church and promised a share in the Holy Spirit who (so

---

* For the titles given to Jesus Christ, see V. Taylor's study, *The Names of Jesus* (London, 1954).
† Mounce, op. cit., pp. 83 f.

prophecy had declared, Joel ii, 28–32) would be given to those who were the new people of God of the End-time.

So the *kerygma* was proclaimed – and with great success, for about three thousand responded to the call and became the Lord's people (ii, 41).

When we come to inquire about the preaching to the Church – what Professor Dodd called *didache* (teaching) – there is far less to go on. We know that the converts on the day of the Church's birth (as Augustine named it) devoted themselves to the Apostles' teaching; and there is at least one tantalizingly brief cameo of a ministry to believers in Acts (xx, 7–12). In 1 Corinthians xiv, 3, 'prophecy' is mentioned as a speaking to men 'for their upbuilding, and encouragement and consolation' (R.S.V.), while xiv, 26 in that Letter speaks of 'instruction', a 'revelation', 'an ecstatic utterance' and its 'interpretation'. All these parts of spoken ministry are acceptable, Paul assures, provided they serve to upbuild the Church. Women may engage in 'prophecy' (1 Corinthians xi, 5), although they should not aspire to an authoritative teaching office (1 Timothy ii, 12).

Much emphasis is placed on the need for instructed Christians (Hebrews v, 11–14; vi, 1 f.; xiii, 7) and Christian leaders are encouraged to give themselves also to their responsible tasks. Many such exhortations are found in Paul's writings, especially in his admonitions to his junior colleagues and their helpers (1 Timothy iv, 6, 13 ff.; v, 17; vi, 2 ff.; 2 Timothy ii, 2; iv, 2, 3; Titus i, 9). The Pauline encouragement to Archippus is especially notable: 'See that you fulfil the ministry which you have received in the Lord' (Colossians iv, 17). In a similar vein, Peter exhorts his readers to diligent service in the Church (1 Peter iv, 10, 11).

God in Christ has given to His people the offices of pastor and teacher, so that all the Church members may attain to mature manhood, to the measure of the stature of Christ in His fulness (Ephesians iv, 11–13; Colossians i, 28; iv, 7; Ephesians iv, 14; Galatians iv, 19).

7

'Concerning the Collection' – Christian Stewardship

Our immediate concern in this chapter is with the New Testament teaching on that part of Christian worship which involves the giving of the Church for the work of God and the furtherance of the Gospel. The rich and ample Old Testament data which relate to 'tithes and offerings' in the Levitical, monarchial and post-exilic periods of the nation's history; and the cultural and historical background of the New Testament allusions to money are not included in our purview.* Our interest is more specific and circumscribed.

A good starting place is in 1 Corinthians xvi, 1–4. This passage contains some important principles of Christian stewardship; and the section falls into the setting of the Church's worship of God.

The opening verses run:

> 'Now concerning the collection for the saints, as I have given order to the churches of Galatia, even so do ye. Upon the first day of the week let every one of you lay by him in store, as God hath prospered him, that there be no gatherings when I come . . .'

The first principle shows clearly the evidence of Christian concern for those who are in distress. The object of the Corinthian Church's contribution was the relief of the poor 'saints' (i.e. Jewish Christians) in Jerusalem, as Romans xv, 26 describes them. Some years prior to the writing of 1 Corinthians, Paul had accepted a measure of responsibility for the poverty-stricken Church at Jerusalem (Acts xi, 27–30); and thereafter had agreed to 'remember' these needy fellow-believers and to

* For this background, see *New Bible Dictionary* (ed. J. D. Douglas: London, 1962 abbreviated hereafter as N.B.D.), under 'Money'; and the standard work of F. W. Madden, *Coins of the Jews* (London, 1881).

bring their continuing claim for help before the Gentile
Churches which, under God, he had established (Galatians ii,
10). The reason for the acute economic distress of the mother-
Church is not exactly known, but many commentators, ancient
and modern, trace its cause to the voluntary 'communism'
which the Jerusalem Christians practised (Acts ii, 44–45; iv,
34–v, 5). This left them with no capital and no resources to
meet the strain of the years ahead. Paul accepted the situation,
and saw in the readiness to help of the Gentile Churches, both
in their prosperity (2 Corinthians viii, 14; ix, 11) and in their
penury (2 Corinthians viii, 2, 3), a powerful piece of evidence
of the unity of the one Church of Jesus Christ; and the rightful claim of necessitous Christians upon their fellow-believers
(Romans xii, 13; xv, 26 f.). The comprehensive admonition of
Galatians vi, 10: 'As we have therefore opportunity, let us do
good unto all men' is given a sharper point and an added
practicality by the words which immediately follow: 'especially
unto them who are of the household of faith'.

Secondly, the giving must be systematic and regular, as verse
2 of 1 Corinthians xvi directs: 'Every Sunday each of you is to
put aside and keep by him a sum in proportion to his gains'
(N.E.B.). Every Church member was expected to set aside a
sum of money, 'as God had prospered him', from his weekly
income. This rubric follows the earlier practice of Acts xi, 29.
Paul hints that he would eventually visit the Church at Corinth
(1 Corinthians xi, 34), and warns now in advance that it will not
do for the money for the 'Fund' to be hurriedly assembled
then. He advises against any 'last-minute rush to get subscrip-
tions in,' as James Moffatt phrases it.* The remedy against this
unseemly policy is for the money to be set aside from the
weekly gains of the believers and kept until it can be collected
and sent off to Jerusalem. So verse 3. In this advice the
Apostle has in mind the claim laid upon the Jews of the Dispersion. Every male Jew over the age of twenty years was required to contribute towards the maintenance of the Temple
and its services. The money was collected at various centres
and taken by responsible agents to the holy city. The term
used in 2 Corinthians viii, 23 in a context which is parallel
with that in 1 Corinthians xvi, 3, 'messengers' (literally
'Apostles', 'delegates', from the Greek *apostoloi*) reproduces
in Greek the exact word which was used of the Jewish officials

* J. Moffatt, *First Epistle of Paul to the Corinthians* (London, 1938).
p. 272.

whose task it was to collect and to bring in the Temple dues and the money for the support of the Rabbinate in Jerusalem.*

Thirdly, we may note that what may have seemed to be a very mundane business – the duty of allocating a sum of cash from the weekly budget – is set in a noble frame by the reference to 'the first day of the week' (verse 2). This is undoubtedly an allusion to the Church's holy day, the day of Christian fellowship in commemoration of the Lord's Resurrection (cf. Revelation i, 10) and the day of the Supper-meal (Acts xx, 7). There are important references to early Christian practices on this day which effectively replaced the Sabbath as the pre-eminent holy-day. Ignatius, writing the early decades of the second century, speaks thus of the new hope in Christ that men may 'no longer live for the Sabbath, but for the Lord's day on which also our life sprang up through Him and His death', in a context which warns against Judaizing.† Compare in the New Testament Colossians ii, 16, 17. Then, there is a clear indication that the Christian 'Sunday' served to perpetuate the festival of the Lord's victory over death in the epistle of Barnabas (about 120 or so, in the reign of the emperor Hadrian, A.D. 117–38): 'Wherefore we also celebrate with gladness the eighth day in which Jesus also rose from the dead, and was made manifest (to the disciples, as in Matthew xxviii, 1 ff.), and ascended into heaven'.‡ Finally, *Didache* xiv, 1 is a witness to the meeting of the Church at the Lord's table on this day: 'On the Lord's day of the Lord come together, break bread and hold Eucharist.' All these references fill out the observance of Christian practices on 'the first day of the week'.

As for the Corinthians' meeting on this day and the reference Paul makes to the offering of money for the 'Fund' are concerned, there may be an additional reason for Paul's recommendation. The first day of the week may have been, as J. Héring suggests,§ pay-day for the people of Corinth. If this is the case, the point is underlined that there was, in his mind, no disparity between the 'secular' and the 'sacred', and no incongruity in the thought that the offering of money is an

---

* See T. W. Manson's discussion, *The Church's Ministry* (London, 1948), p. 38.

† Ignatius, *Magnesians*, chaps. viii–x.

‡ Barnabas xv, 9.

§ J. Héring, *First Epistle of Saint Paul to the Corinthians* (London, E.T., 1962), p. 183.

integral part of Christian worship. Money which had been
honestly gained in the toil of the week is to be brought to the
assembly of the Church and thus made part of the Sunday
worship. This seems implicit in the Apostolic directive; and is
confirmed by the practice of Christian worship in the next
century. Justin Martyr – to whose account of the Church's
worship at Rome in the middle of the second century we have
already referred – remarks how 'each member who is well-to-
do and willing gives as he pleases, and the amount is deposited
with the presiding minister (in the Church)'.* But for the
Pauline Churches, it was everyone – rich and poor (compare
1 Corinthians i, 26; xi, 19) – who was invited to share the
responsibility of Christian stewardship.

New Testament Teaching Concerning Money

With the background of the Corinthians passage behind us,
we may go on to inspect more closely the New Testament's
teaching on money, if we are rightly to appreciate the meaning
of Christian giving in the setting of worship. Three observa-
tions may be made.

(i) *The Importance of Money*

For all its emphasis on the spirituality and transcendence of
God's relationship with man, and man's response to God in
the offering of himself (Romans xii, 1, 2), the New Testament
never allows us to forget that we live in this 'present world'
(2 Timothy iv, 10; 1 Corinthians vii, 31) and in the rough-
and-tumble of life. The Gospel does not miraculously transport us to some spiritual Shangri-la where all is bliss and ease
and unsullied pleasure. Our calling as Christians is to be dis-
charged in the world of the market-place, the business-house
and the farm – to use the terms which belong primarily to the
commercial ethos of the first century. (In twentieth century
terms we should read instead such vocations as are conducted
in the Departmental store, the Bank and on the shop-floor of
the factory.) These places of work are frequently mentioned
in the Gospels; and some, more exotic occupations are referred to in the Letters (e.g., the coppersmith, the lawyer, the
city treasurer; 2 Timothy iv, 14; Titus iii, 13; Romans xvi, 23).
We are left in no doubt that New Testament Christians were

* Justin Martyr, *First Apology*, chap. lxvii.

not encouraged to withdraw from the world to a life of secluded contemplation; rather their high calling in Christ is set in the midst of a busy, struggling, striving, competitive world, the counterpart of which we can see today in the office, shipyard and workshop.* There are positive injunctions against sloth and unconcern with social issues (2 Thessalonians iii, 10–13) and, at least by inference, it is hinted that man has to work in order to keep alive (2 Timothy ii, 6). Certainly, no premium is set on laziness and irresponsibility in the interest of a supposed, but spurious, 'spirituality' (Matthew xxv, 14–30; 1 Thessalonians v, 14).

In New Testament teaching, money is recognized as a means of exchange and livelihood; and every possible stress is placed on the need of diligence and conscientiousness in the Christian's daily work. These exhortations are found in sections of the epistles which are labelled by scholars 'Household Codes', which supply converts with rules and regulations for everyday living (see Ephesians vi, 5 ff.; Colossians iii, 22–24; Titus ii, 1–10; 1 Peter ii, 13 ff.).† As many of the newly-converted would doubtless be members of the slave-class, it was much to the point that Apostolic instruction should offer some guidance to them for their responsibility and relationships to their masters.

But there is a deeper reason for this call to honest employ and best effort. We worship God in the path of our daily tasks; and the offering to Him of all good craftsmanship and dedicated skill, with the best output of mind and hand, is as much a part of our Christian 'cult' as the hymn-singing and devotion of our Church services. Hence the typically Pauline addition to what may appear as a pre-Christian exhortation, 'work heartily': 'as serving the Lord' (Colossians iii, 23).

It is the collection, given and received in the name of Christ the Carpenter,‡ which joins together these two aspects. The gift is 'sanctified'; and the worship is 'concretized', as the

* Among many recent books which take up the theme of the Christian's attitude to work and wealth, we may mention D. L. Munby's *God and the Rich Society* (Oxford, 1961).

† Essay II in E. G. Selwyn's *First Epistle of St. Peter* (London, 1947) considers these passages in detail.

‡ Alan Richardson writes: 'The tragedy of our age is that the working classes of the world should have turned their eyes away from the workman of Nazareth and opened their minds to the false gospel of the bourgeois "scribbler in the British Museum",' art. 'Work', *A Theological Wordbook of the Bible* (ed. A. Richardson, London, 1950), pp. 286 f.

fruit of our daily work is brought and offered. The later Church attached much importance to this aspect of public worship, especially at the Communion service when the produce of an agricultural community was presented and offered as a token of man's thanksgiving to God.*

(ii) *The Menace of Money*

In the teaching of the New Testament writers, however, the emphasis falls more strongly on the dangers which the possession and wrong use of money present. Money may be gained and used – and there is some tacit approval of the principles which underlie John Wesley's famous sermon on 'The Use of Money', based on Luke xvi, 9† – but it may also be misused and worshipped. In the terrifying possibility that money may become our god, Jesus and His Apostles find the perilous snare of covetousness. This sin may be defined as the spirit of grasping greed and acquisitiveness, the insatiable longing for more of material possessions and a consequent lack of contentment and absence of trust in God our Father who has promised to supply all needful things to His children (Matthew vi, 32). There is an expressive Greek word, *pleonexia* for this outlook on life; and Paul gives it its right description when he writes: 'covetousness (*pleonexia*), which is idolatry' (Colossians iv, 5). The consequences of living under the grip of a covetous spirit are set forth with startling clarity throughout the New Testament (see Mark x, 24, 25; Luke xii, 13–34; Acts v, 1–10; viii, 20; xxiv, 26; 1 Timothy vi, 9, 10, R.S.V. which reads 'Those who desire to be rich fall into . . . a snare'; 2 Timothy iv, 10; and, drawing upon an Old Testament illustration, 2 Peter ii, 15 rebukes those who 'have followed the way of Balaam, the son of Beor, who loved gain from wrongdoing').

Our Lord's characteristic term for money (in this context) is 'Mammon' (Matthew vi, 24; Luke xvi, 13). This is a general Aramaic word for wealth; but He personified it and treated it as a god which seeks to claim and command a man's allegiance. Yet, when we bring our money into the Lord's house, and present it in worship, we thereby declare that all

* Cf. A. F. Walls, art, 'A Primitive Christian Harvest Thanksgiving', *Theology*, lviii, 1955, pp. 336 ff.

† In his *Sermons on Several Occasions*, No. 50 (First series, published in 1771).

wealth is from Him (see Haggai ii, 8), is subservient to Him
(1 Corinthians vii, 30, 31), and is offered back to Him in
gratitude (James i, 17).

(iii) *The Consecration of Money*

This leads us on to our consideration of the consecration of
money. As temptation may be resisted and overcome in
Christ, so the ensnaring power of money may be broken and
the spirit of possessiveness may be neutralized. Thus what was
a potential curse may be turned into a blessing – which is a
familiar Old Testament thought (Deuteronomy xxiii, 5;
Nehemiah xiii, 2). This is precisely the meaning of our Christian giving in worship.

While there is a 'world-denying' strain in the Gospels, which
would bid us 'sell all' and practise asceticism (Matthew xix,
21; cf. Acts iv, 36, 37; 2 Corinthians vi, 10), there is an equally
insistent 'world-affirming' call which bids us to 'do good' with
our money (1 Timothy vi, 17–19) and to employ it for the
glory of God and the service of our fellow-men and fellow-
Christians in their distress (Luke xvi, 9; 2 Corinthians viii,
13, 14; Galatians vi, 10; 1 John iii, 17, 18). God is glorified in
this way as though the gifts had been presented to Him
directly (Philippians iv, 18; Hebrews xiii, 16). If Judas Iscariot,
who loved base gain (Matthew xxvi, 14–16; John xii, 1–8,
R.S.V.) is condemned and held up as a warning in the New
Testament, Joseph of Arimathaea, a 'rich man' (Matthew
xxvii, 57–60; John xix, 38–42) is commended and set forth
for emulation. There is also the case of another Joseph, sur-
named Barnabas, who sold his land and brought the money
to the Apostles in order to help forward the missionary expansion of the Gospel (Acts iv, 36, 37). This story admirably
illustrates the consecration of money as it is freely offered in
the service of the work of God and His Kingdom.

In a recent, powerful sermon,* Dr. R. L. Small has told
how 'one "pawky" Scots elder used to say, "Money isn't
everything; but it's very handy to go a message with! " '. He
comments: 'It is indeed – it is handy to go a message with
on the Master's business; it is handy to express our concern
for the coming of His Kingdom. The using and giving of our
money is often the only means we have of showing how much

* R. L. Small, *No Uncertain Sound* (Edinburgh, 1963), in a sermon
entitled 'The Clink of Coins', pp. 72 f.

we care for need, known and realized. The money I give to my church constitutes, whether I realize it or not, in terms of my total budget, the measure of my love and gratitude; it tells how much, or how little, Christ means to me.'

To this timely reminder of the place of money in Church life, one rider may be added. The offering must be made in the right spirit (see Matthew vi, 1–4; Mark xii, 41–44), with a desire to please Him and not to impress our fellows with our ostentatious generosity, and with a real concern to help on His work by our gifts.

In these ways, our worship is shown to be real, for it is easy to *say* that the Lord is our God and that our desire is directed to Him and to those in need. There are some stinging words of rebuke of this 'disembodied help' – see James ii, 15–17; 1 John iii, 17, 18. The acid test is not what we say, but what we do; not what we promise in words, but what we actually give in money. True worship is not lip-service, but the prelude to action in service and in the world. The taking of the collection saves us from both unreality and sentimentalism which thinks of Christian worship as merely pious exercises, and a philanthropy and social concern which thinks only on the horizontal plane of helping one's neighbour. Christian worship is realistic and positive – as hard as the coins we put into the plate; yet is set within a theological frame of reference which sees the needy neighbour whom we seek to help as one for whom Christ died and whom He would reclaim. Moreover, he has a claim upon our love and sympathy because he is more than a fellow human being; he is a child of God in the making.

Seven Principles of Christian Stewardship

If we seek for a systematic presentation of the New Testament teaching on the Christian's attitude to money, it is to the two chapters viii and ix in 2 Corinthians that we shall naturally turn. At least seven principles of Christian stewardship are to be seen in this section, which treats of the Corinthians' responsibility for the 'collection for the saints' (in 1 Corinthians xvi, 1 ff.).

(i) As a didactic background Paul places the amazing and constant gifts of God to His people (ix, 10, 11) in His provision for all their needs, and especially in the gift of His only Son to a lost race of men. The Lord's self-effacement and self-giving prove His grace and this sets the tone of the Apostle's entire discussion (viii, 9; ix, 15). Our giving to God and His work is always to be viewed in the light of the Incarnation and humiliation of the Lord of glory who gave Himself in utter self-abandon in life and in death, 'betrothing Himself for ever to the human race, for better, for worse, for richer, for poorer, in sickness and in health'.*

(ii) The chiefest offering a man can give in response is the committal of his own life. The Apostle has already made this deduction in chapter v, 15: 'He died for all, that those who live might live no longer for themselves but for Him who for their sake died and rose again'. Now he goes on, in viii, 5, to apply it to the human situation: 'but first they gave themselves to the Lord'. Such a dedication shows itself in a corresponding practical interest in the work of the Gospel, for he proceeds: 'and to us by the will of God'.

(iii) All Christian giving is prompted by divine grace (viii, 1; ix, 14), yet it is voluntary (ix, 5, 7); eager (viii, 4.); cheerful (viii, 2; ix, 7), i.e. not inhibited by wrong motives such as unwillingness or cold duty; sacrificial (viii, 2, 3; ix, 6, 11). The Macedonian Christians gave at great cost because they were in the grip of a financial depression, as the opening of chapter viii makes quite clear.

(iv) Further qualities mentioned as exemplifying the grace of a generous spirit (viii, 7) are: according to one's ability (viii, 11–14); with a sense of equality (viii, 14) which means that those who have should share with those who are needy. Fair shares all round, is the Pauline advice; and out of a genuine love for those in distress (viii, 8).

(v) God is no man's debtor. As we do our part (viii, 10, 11), it is in the confidence that His providence will supply our needs (ix, 8). He challenges us through the example of others (viii, 1, 8; ix, 2); and our ready response to the call of Christian duty and the need of others will spur our fellow-believers too (ix, 2).

(vi) Christian stewards must be fair and open in their financial dealings, and scrupulously honest and above-board (viii, 20, 21).

(vii) Finally, such disinterested concern for the welfare of others creates a bond of love between giver and recipient; and calls forth the praise of God (ix, 12–14).

* W. Russell Maltby's famous phrase, *Christ and His Cross* (London, 1963 ed.), p. 70.

We notice from this section with what care and attention to detail Paul treats the subject of the Church's monetary responsibility. He abhors and rebukes all that is slipshod and haphazard; and equally all that is given in a mechanical and unthinking way. Hence the patient instruction in these chapters.

No act of public worship can mean so much or so little as the giving and receiving of our gifts in God's house. If we offer our collection unthinkingly and formally, the act is devoid of all spiritual significance and warmth. But, if we see the collection as an integral part of corporate worship and anchor it thus firmly in the total response we make to the Gospel news, then it takes on a new, richer meaning; and the dedication of our money becomes the outward and visible sign of the inward and spiritual grace of a thankful heart. Like all true worship, the offering is sacramental.

8

The Gospel Sacraments – Baptism in the Teaching of Jesus

'Our Lord Jesus Christ hath knit together a company of new people by sacraments, most few in number, most easy to be kept, most excellent in signification.' This famous statement by Augustine, the fifth century bishop of Hippo in North Africa* (whose statement is quoted in the 1553 version of the Thirty-nine Articles) reminds us of some important principles of the sacramental aspects of Christian worship.

We learn that the observance of the Gospel ordinances is no human invention, but is rather our response to the divine command. Such obedience, however, is no irksome duty and unpleasant task to be performed because it is imposed upon us by a tyrannical authority. Quite the contrary. Human obedience is an occasion of glad acceptance of God's will, for 'His commandments are not burdensome' (1 John v, 3, R.S.V.). Moreover, it is no meaningless ritual we perform when we observe His ordinances, no piece of ecclesiastical mumbo-jumbo; sacramental practice is full of Gospel truth, and is intended for our enrichment and edification.

Our immediate concern is with the worship of the New Testament Church. This delimiting of our interest means that we may pass over the meaning of the term 'sacrament', and the significance of the sacraments in present-day discussion and ecumenical debate. Our task is much simpler. We have to inquire into the New Testament teaching in as impartial a way as possible, although we are under no illusion that a completely objective approach to this controversial subject is possible, after centuries of Christian history and disputation. It was a wise teacher who remarked that one can only say what the Scriptures *mean* when one has first said what they

---

* Augustine, *Ep.* 54: 'sacramentis numero paucissimis, observatione facillimis, significatione praestantissimis'.

meant. In other words, we all – irrespective of denominational or confessional loyalty and conviction – need constantly to go back to the fountain-head of the New Testament – or, to change the metaphor, to test our present-day beliefs and practices by what we find written in the records of the early Church. Certain issues relating to the central Gospel truths are taught and admit of no compromise; there are, equally, marginal issues which may be legitimately discussed between Christians with a resultant divergence of opinion and practice. The really difficult and delicate matter is to decide which belief and/or practice belongs to the category of 'things essential' and which to 'things doubtful'. But the great *desideratum* is that all things should be viewed in a total context, and the spirit of love, not divisiveness, prevail.

The sacramental teachings on Baptism and the Lord's Supper have, alas, been the source of much acrimonious debate. The following chapters are not aimed at stirring up fresh contention, but rather at setting down what seems to be the New Testament picture. We turn to a relatively simple matter, to begin: Jesus' own words about baptism and His attitude to the rite, both in practice and command.

Introductory

The use of water in religious ceremonial is age-old. Ritual ablutions are very prominent in the Old Testament, both in the cases of religious impurity (in Leviticus and Numbers xix), and in those instances when a ritual washing was part of the ceremony which a person practised as he approached God (e.g., the high priest in Exodus xl, 12–15; Leviticus viii; Numbers viii). But, in addition to these ceremonial acts, the need for *moral* cleansing is brought out in a number of graphically worded texts:

> 'Wash you, make you clean; put away the evil of your doings from before mine eyes; cease to do evil'
>
> (Isaiah i, 16).

> 'Then will I sprinkle clean water upon you; and ye shall be clean: from all your filthiness, and from all your idols, will I cleanse you'
>
> (Ezekiel xxxvi, 25).

'In that day there shall be a fountain opened to the house of David and to the inhabitants of Jerusalem for sin and for uncleanness'

(Zechariah xiii, 1).

'Wash me, and I shall be whiter than snow'

(Psalm li, 7).

Some of these verses look forward to the day when God will renew His people, and are a tacit admission that outer cleanliness and ritual purification are not enough. We may see this admission illustrated in Isaiah iv, 2–6; Ezekiel xxxvi, 25 ff., 33; xxxvii, 23; and Jeremiah xxxiii, 8.

The more spiritually sensitive among Israel's people looked for a time of national renewal and hope. It is therefore not surprising that some 'sectarian' groups (the Essenes are the best-known examples*) made much use of baptismal lustrations in order to secure a holy people, who would be clean, both ceremonially and morally, and thus be in a fit state to herald the dawn of a new age and a purified Temple worship. The recently discovered documents of the Covenanters of Qumran give some vivid instances of this fervent hope, and of the serious preparations which they made to fit themselves for the part they would play in God's new order. But the sectaries of Qumran knew that water alone could not cleanse the soul; the Holy Spirit working within the community must bring about the essential purification.† This awareness among the people of the Dead Sea scrolls is one of the most important pieces of evidence of a yearning for spiritual renewal and cleansing, which pointed forward to the fulfilment in the Gospel.

But there is another line of development which was also preparing the Jews of the first centuries B.C. and A.D. for the advent of the Gospel and its accompanying ceremonial acts.

* The basic account is given by Josephus, *Wars of the Jews*, Book II, 8, 5.

† See *The Community Rule*, iv:
'He will cleanse him of all wicked deeds with the spirit of holiness; like purifying waters He will shed upon him the spirit of truth (to cleanse him) of all abomination and falsehood' (Vermès, *The Dead Sea Scrolls in English*, pp. 77 f. Cf. ibid., iii. 6–9 (Vermès, op. cit. p. 75).

There is a discussion of this teaching in N. A. Dahl's essay, 'The Origin of Baptism', *Festschrift* for S. Mowinckel (Oslo, 1955), pp. 36–52, espec. p. 45.

This is the practice of proselyte baptism.* This ceremony made it possible for a Gentile to enter the fold of Judaism. The candidate was required to accept the demands of the Law; to receive circumcision, if he were a male; and later to be baptized in the presence of witnesses as a prelude to the offering of sacrifice. The entire procedure was a means of entry into the new religion; but the 'point of no return' came in the moment when the proselyte emerged from the water. Thenceforth he was regarded as a newly-born son of Abraham's family. 'When he has been baptized, he is regarded in all respects as an Israelite,' commented the Rabbis.† A new life awaited him.

Both sectarian and proselyte baptism are important for an understanding of a character whose baptismal practice marks the beginning of the Gospel story: John the baptizer. It is possible that the exordium of Mark's Gospel should read: 'the beginning of the Good News of Jesus . . . was John the Baptist's preaching of a baptism of repentance'. This view, adopted by some of the Greek Fathers of the Church and, in modern times, by C. H. Turner,‡ would find confirmation in Acts i, 22; x, 37 and xiii, 24, 25, all of which place the baptizing ministry as the frontispiece of the ministry of Him in whom the Gospel was actualized. These verses focus attention upon John's distinctive practice, for of the many features of this Messianic herald's work none is more important than his baptizing his fellow-Jews in preparation for the coming of God's Rule in Jesus; and in that record of his baptisms no single baptism is more significant than his receiving and baptizing his cousin, Jesus of Nazareth (Mark i, 7–11; Matthew iii, 13–17; Luke iii, 21–23; John i, 24–34). This event provides us – as it provided the first generations of Christian believers – with a fixed starting point in regard to the full import of the Christian ordinance.

* On proselyte baptism see the carefully documented essays by A. Gilmore in *Christian Baptism* (ed. A. Gilmore: London, 1959); and W. F. Flemington, *The New Testament Doctrine of Baptism* (London, 1948), chap. 1.

† D. Daube, *The New Testament and Rabbinic Judaism* (London, 1956), pp. 110 f.

‡ C. H. Turner in *A New Commentary on Holy Scripture* (edd. C. Gore and others, London, 1928) ad loc.

(i) *He submitted to baptism*

The account in Matthew iii, 13–17 is not easy to interpret; and there is some evidence from the apocryphal gospels that the early Church was puzzled by the fact that the sinless Lord should submit to a baptism 'for the remission of sins' (Mark i, 4, 5).* The difficulty is eased if, with T. W. Manson,† we recall that the people who came to John's baptism did so with a great variety of motives. Some came with a burden of sinfulness; others came because they were convinced that John was the herald of a new age; and others were impelled by a zeal for Israel and Israel's God. And John's most illustrious candidate saw in the revival movement on Jordan's banks the sign that His public ministry was about to begin. He came, therefore, to identify Himself openly with John as 'a man sent from God' (John i, 6), the predestined herald of Messiah's coming (Matthew xi, 6–15; Luke vii, 24–30; Mark ix, 9–13); and also with the people whom He came to save (John i, 11). He would not hold Himself aloof from them. From the outset of His ministry to its climax on the Cross, He was 'numbered among the transgressors' as He fulfilled all righteousness (Matthew iii, 15; cf. Matthew xxi, 32: 'for John came unto you in the way of righteousness' and Luke vii, 29, which are both important references to the place of John in the economy of God's salvation) in an acceptance of God's purpose for His Messianic life.

This understanding of the baptism of our Lord is not guesswork, but is confirmed by the attesting signs which accompanied the event. The signs were three in number: the opened heavens; the descent of the dove; and the Father's voice.

The 'rent heavens' must be understood on a Jewish background; for in the Old Testament this metaphor can only mean that God has broken into human history (so Isaiah lxiv, 1; Psalm xviii, 9, cxliv, 5). The dove is symbolic of the Spirit of God in His work at creation's dawn (Genesis i, 2). Now,

---

* E.g. in the *Gospel of the Hebrews* as quoted by Jerome:
'Behold the Lord's mother and brethren said to Him, John the Baptist is baptizing unto the remission of sins: let us go and be baptized by him.

   Then He said to them, What sin have I done that I should go and be baptized by him? – unless perchance this very thing that I have said is a sin of ignorance.'

† T. W. Manson, *The Servant-Messiah* (Cambridge, 1956), pp. 46 f.

at the new creation (2 Corinthians iv, 4–6), He comes again to hover over the water. The mention of the 'heavenly voice' takes us back to the Jewish idea that when God speaks in heaven, His voice – the daughter of a voice, the Rabbis said – is heard on earth.* And the Rabbis always associated this with the declaration of the Hebrew Old Testament. So, true to form, the Father's witness to His Son is couched in Scriptural language. 'Thou art my beloved Son' (Psalm ii, 7): 'with thee I am well pleased' (Isaiah xlii, 1) – a striking combination of verses which portray Jesus as the Messianic Son and Suffering Servant,† with an underlying motif in the wording which recalls Abraham's description of Isaac in Genesis xxii.‡

If His baptism marks the opening of His ministry, the accompanying signs will show the way in which that ministry will be exercised. The pattern is that of Isaiah's Servant-Son (the one Greek title *pais* covers both terms) who by a ministry of service and obedience will atone for His people's sins (Isaiah liii in the light of Mark x, 45; and there is some evidence that, in Rabbinic thought, the 'sacrifice' of Isaac was envisaged as atoning for sin).§ The path to Calvary runs from Jordan's river.

(ii) *He sanctioned baptism*

There is no record in the Synoptic Gospels that our Lord or His disciples actually baptized. But that they did so is clearly indicated by John iii, 22–26; iv, 1, 2. There are some points which tell strongly in favour of our acceptance of the Johannine tradition. The first is that the Synoptics are concerned mainly with the Lord's ministry in Galilee, and pass over the ministry in the south, although they imply it. The

---

* For this Rabbinic notion of *Bath Qol* see I. Abrahams, *Studies in Pharisaism and the Gospels:* First series (Cambridge, 1917), pp. 47 f. Two examples of Jewish ideas are interesting. *Sanhedrin* 11a explains the idea in terms of an echo : 'as when a man strikes a powerful blow and a second sound is heard'. In *Berakoth* 3a it is compared to the moaning of a dove.

† For this identification, see O. Cullmann, *Baptism in the New Testament* (London, E. T. 1950), pp. 16 ff. and W. Zimmerli and J. Jeremias, *The Servant of God* (London, E. T. 1957), pp. 80 ff.

‡ This factor is suggestively introduced by G. Vermès in the chapter 'Redemption and Genesis xxii' in his *Scripture and Tradition in Judaism* (Leiden, 1961), pp. 222 f.

§ Cf. Vermès, op. cit., pp. 202 ff. for the Targumic interpretation of the story of Isaac in the light of Isaiah liii.

proof of this inference lies in Matthew xxiii, 37 = Luke xiii, 34: 'How often would I have gathered thy children' seems inc ubitably to point to many visits to the holy city. John has evidently preserved some reliable traditions which relate to the early ministry in Judea as well as some subsequent visits to Jerusalem, and is at pains to describe these in some detail. A growing body of modern scholarship is finding an important place for the historical traditions of the opening chapters of John's Gospel which record an early ministry in Judea.*

Then, there is the confirmation of the importance of a practice of baptism in this initial stage of the ministry, about which W. F. Flemington has written. 'If baptism were practised (in this early stage of the public ministry of Jesus) with the approval of Jesus, it becomes easier to explain why, immediately after Pentecost, baptism took its place as the normal rite of entry into the Christian community.'†

And, thirdly, we may keep in mind the close of the ministry, when the risen Christ charged His disciples to go and baptize. This command, about which we shall be concerned below, is congruous with what had gone before if, in fact, baptism was no novelty; but a feature of the work of Jesus and His followers 'in the days of his flesh'.

It seems fairly clear, then, that the Lord's own *imprimatur* was upon this rite, although we must remain in some doubt as to whether He actually performed the baptismal action. Sanction of baptism does not necessarily mean that the person who sanctions the rite must himself administer it, as we learn from the cases of Peter (in Acts x, 47, 48) and Paul who had to treat baptism with some reserve at Corinth because there was a misunderstanding of the importance of the one who administered it (so 1 Corinthians i, 14–17).‡

(iii) *He interpreted baptism*

Although the practice of baptism as an integral part of the public mission of Jesus is unrecorded in the first three Gospels,

* The 'newer' assessment is outlined by J. A. T. Robinson in his essay contributed to *The Roads Converge* (ed. P. Gardiner-Smith: London, 1963); and in greater detail by C. H. Dodd, *Historical Tradition in the Fourth Gospel* (Cambridge, 1963), pp. 248 ff.

† W. F. Flemington, op. cit., p. 31.

‡ For the local background to the Corinthian misunderstanding, see J. Héring, *The First Epistle of Saint Paul to the Corinthians*, (London, E. T. 1962), p. 7.

the word (used in a figurative sense) is twice found upon the lips of the Master. And both are significant, for both are explanations of His Passion (Luke xii, 50; Mark x, 38, 39).

The second saying, 'Are you able to be baptized with the baptism that I am baptized with?' is associated with His drinking the cup of suffering. This latter expression is a common one for intense human suffering and woe (see Psalm lxxv, 8; Isaiah li, 17 ff.; Jeremiah xlix, 12; Lamentations iv, 21; Ezekiel xxiii, 31 ff.). In a similar way, the thought of baptism suggests the experience of drowning under the waters of great grief and anguish (see Psalms xlii, 7, lxix, 2, 15; cxxiv, 4–5; Isaiah xliii, 2).

If this is the background of the Lord's words about His impending death on the Cross, the saying of Luke xii, 50 ('I have a baptism to undergo. What tension I suffer, till it is all over!', Moffatt's translation) shows us how the Lord in His true humanity reacted, as at Gethsemane, to the horror of sin-bearing which loomed before Him. But there may be another meaning. Let us recall that the Old Testament looked forward to God's renewal of His people in terms of a baptismal renewing. Jesus may thus have foreseen that His death and victory would usher in the Kingdom of God, and inaugurate the final chapter of God's dealing with men. At all events, He clearly interpreted His death as a baptismal action, full of deep significance both for Himself and His Church. It cannot be without an intended connexion that St. Paul uses exactly these two terms of baptism and death, in reverse order, as he interprets Christian baptism as a sharing of Christ's death and resurrection (Romans vi, 3 ff.; Colossians ii, 12).*

(iv) *He commanded baptism*

Matthew xxviii, 19, 20 contain what are among the most important – and the most controverted – words of Jesus Christ. The risen Lord, possessed of all authority, bids His disciples to go into all the world with a commission which includes 'baptizing in the name of the Father, and of the Son, and of the Holy Spirit'. The significance of this dominical utterance, if taken at its face value, is rightly assessed by

* This observation derives from E. Stauffer whose sentence 'Jesus nennt sein Sterben eine Taufe: Paulus hinwiederum nennt unsere Taufe ein Sterben' (*Die Theologie des Neuen Testaments:* Stuttgart, 1948 ed., p. 130 f.) I have not been able to trace in the English translation *New Testament Theology* (London, 1955).

R. E. O. White in the words: 'The passage adds one totally new note, perhaps unique in the New Testament: that the *practice* of baptism by the church (as distinct from its *acceptance* by the baptized) is an act of obedience to divine command. The unique circumstances of this great utterance, the association with the world-wide commission, the link with the requirement of absolute obedience, and the attachment of the unforgettable promise of the Master's presence to the end of the age, all lend a solemnity and power to the saying which reflect on to the baptismal reference a significance even greater than the simple command itself.'*

All sorts of objections have been brought against this text – literary, textual, historical and theological; and there is no consensus of agreement among the commentators. P. W. Evans's important Tyndale Lecture, *Sacraments in the New Testament*† will acquaint the student with the important issues which this passage evokes. James Denney makes an important point when he comments on the congruity of the Lord's command to baptize both with what has gone before in the Gospels and with what will follow in the other New Testament literature and the practice of the Apostolic Church.‡ Flemington agrees with this reasoning (although he is more sceptical about the veracity of the actual words of Jesus in the text), and finds the key in the authority of Jesus which the early Church claimed as they, following the Pentecostal preaching, began immediately to baptize the converts. Such an authority must go back to some dominical word, and this word, we may hold, lies in Matthew xxviii. Thus, we may continue to see in these words at the end of Matthew 'a supreme expression of the Christian belief that baptism is no human rite, but rests upon an authority no other than that of Jesus himself'.§

It will be necessary, finally, to examine the objection which many scholars find cogent. Flemington, in particular, fastens upon this, after having shown that textual and literary arguments brought against the authenticity of Matthew xxviii, 19 f. are indecisive. The root of the matter is found in the disparity between the baptismal formulas in Acts and the Pauline

* R. E. O. White, art. 'Baptism in the Synoptic Gospels', *Christian Baptism* (ed. A. Gilmore: London, 1959), p. 112.
† P. W. Evans, *Sacraments in the New Testament* (London, 1947).
‡ J. Denney, *The Death of Christ* (London, 1907), p. 74. This defence of Matthew xxviii enables Denney later (op. cit. p. 84) to declare: 'There is nothing in Christianity more primitive than the Sacraments.'
§ W. F. Flemington, op. cit., p. 129.

Letters and the use of the Trinitarian name here. 'If he (the Lord Jesus) had uttered the command as it stands written here, could baptism "in the name of the Lord Jesus" ever have been so usual as the references in the Acts and the Pauline Epistles would suggest?'*

He correctly regards the expedient of regarding the term, 'in the name of the Lord (Jesus)' as an abbreviation of the sacred formula of the Trinity as an evasion of the difficulty. But he fails to consider the explanation offered by G. F. Moore,† which we shall now summarize.

That there is a difference in the baptismal forms used in the Apostolic Church and as recorded in Matthew xxviii cannot be denied. But regard must be had to the historical circumstance of the documents. The clue to the mystery may be found in just the different historical situations presupposed in Matthew and Acts. The baptisms in the Acts of the Apostles in ii, 38; viii, 16, x, 48 are those of Jews or Jewish 'God-fearers' or people who had been brought under the influence of the Jewish faith. Acts xix, 5 which tells of the baptisms at Ephesus of twelve or so men who were baptized 'in the name of the Lord Jesus' is no exception, for they had previously known the baptismal instruction of John the Baptist (verse 3). The situation envisaged in Matthew xxviii, however, is quite distinct and has in view the Gentile mission and the bringing in of those people who had no background of monotheistic belief. For such, a baptism in the name of the Triune God and a consequent belief in the Father, the Son and the Holy Spirit would be appropriate and necessary, as we have seen in regard to the later practice of the Church when a Trinitarian creed was confessed at baptism. For converted Jews, however, as in the opening chapters of Acts and in some of Paul's missionary work, the simple declaration of Jesus as Messiah and Lord was the important thing.

This explanation looks simple and compelling, but it should not be pressed too far; and it leaves largely untouched the difficulty of Paul's use of baptismal forms ('in the name of the Lord Jesus') in such predominantly Gentile-Christian Churches as Corinth (cf. 1 Corinthians vi, 11 in the light of xii, 2) and Galatia (Galatians iii, 27 in the light of iv, 8, 9). We should then agree with the following conclusion: 'Dog-

* W. F. Flemington, op. cit., p. 108.
† G. F. Moore, *Judaism in the First Three Centuries of the Christian Era* (Cambridge, Mass., 1927–30), Vol. I, pp. 188 f.

matism is out of place, but there seems no convincing argument to prevent our accepting the closing words of Matthew as conveying the meaning of Jesus with no less confidence than attaches to almost any other word or deed attributed to Him; or to preclude our believing that the apostolic church was fundamentally right in concluding that thus and thus the risen Lord would have her do'.*

* R. E. O. White, art. cit., p. 113. See the similar conclusion reached after a careful examination of the evidence by G. R. Beasley-Murray, *Baptism in the New Testament* (London, 1962), pp. 77–92.

Note.—The omission of any reference in the text to Mark x, 13–16 and parallels which record the Blessing of the Children is not an oversight. The present writer cannot persuade himself that, in spite of the arguments therefor by O. Cullmann, op. cit., pp. 25 ff., 76 ff., and J. Jeremias, *Infant Baptism in the First Four Centuries* (London, E. T., 1960), this passage has any direct bearing on New Testament baptismal practice. The *Auseinandersetzung* between Jeremias and K. Aland hardly touches the New Testament question, except at the point of the disputed meaning of 'Household baptisms' (see Jeremias' rejoinder in *The Origins of Infant Baptism*, London, E. T., 1963, pp. 12 ff., 76 ff.).

9

The Apostolic Practice
of Baptism

Introduction

Peter's sermon on the day of Pentecost ended with a rapier thrust which pierced the heart of the hearers. 'Brethren, what shall we do?' was the immediate reaction on their part to all that he had told them of the life, death and resurrection of Jesus the Messiah. And the reply of the Apostle was no less immediate and direct: 'Repent, and be baptized every one of you in the name of Jesus Christ for the forgiveness of sins; and you shall receive the gift of the Holy Spirit' (Acts ii, 37, 38). This recommendation was received and acted upon (Acts ii, 41); and about three thousand persons entered the fellowship of the nascent Church through the gateway of repentance and faith, expressed outwardly by baptism. Augustine's description of the day of Pentecost as the *dies natalis*, or birthday, of the Church of Christ is justified, therefore, if we think of the Church in its societary aspect.

We have already seen in the previous chapter that baptism in water was no new thing. Peter was preaching to fellow-Jews who would have been familiar with proselyte baptism. This latter ceremony had emphasized that a Gentile could be cleansed from sin and made a partaker of all the blessings of the covenant with Israel. In an immeasurably greater and richer way, baptism 'in the name of the Lord Jesus' spoke of new life in the Messianic age and a share in the inheritance of the new Israel, the people of God (Galatians vi, 16). It is worth while setting down the meaning of Christian baptism as the record in the Acts of the Apostles throws light upon it before we turn to the more systematic teaching of St. Paul.

I. *Baptism in the Acts of the Apostles*

The following are the salient points of the baptismal practice in the Acts.

(i) Baptism was administered 'in the name of Jesus Christ' (Acts ii, 38; x, 48), or 'into the name of the Lord Jesus' (Acts viii, 16; xix, 5). Much discussion has been evoked by the reference to the 'name' in these contexts and in Matthew xxviii, 19. Various translations, such as 'belonging to (the Lord) Jesus' or 'dedicating the person to Him' in baptism have been offered, partly on the ground that the phrase is a technical term, used in Hellenistic banking, to denote that a sum of money is placed 'to the credit of' another person.* Applied to the Christian rite, this means that when a man is baptized he is thought of as passing into the ownership of Another to whom he henceforth belongs.

Acts xxii, 16 suggests a further thought. It would imply that the name of Jesus was invoked by the baptizand in the act of his baptism; or even (on the strength of James ii, 7 and, by inference, 1 Corinthians i, 13–15) that the name of Jesus Christ was called over the candidate as he made his baptismal profession. Romans x, 9 is often appealed to in this context, as we have seen earlier.

At all events, we may be sure that baptism in the Lord's name meant at least that the rite was seen as a confession of Christ and an act of submission to His authority, expressed not in word only but by an obedience to His will and a deliberate dedication to His service and lordship. 'The believer was baptized "for the sake of" the Lord Jesus and made over to Him.'†

(ii) Baptism is connected with repentance (Acts ii, 38) and the offer of forgiveness (Acts ii, 38; cf. xxii, 16). Likewise, it is associated with the gift of the Spirit (Acts ii, 38; cf. x, 44–48), although there is no strict order of sequence. Sometimes the Holy Spirit is given with baptism; at other times baptism follows the descent of the Spirit (x, 44 ff.). And we may note (for our admonition) that there is no automatic process or magical formula which guarantees the bestowal of the Spirit, or which necessarily implies that all who were baptized in water received the spiritual counterpart in the gift of the

---

* See A. Oepke's art, in Kittel's *Theological Dictionary of the New Testament* (Grand Rapids: E. T., 1964), under 'Baptize'. Vol. I, p. 539.

† G. R. Beasley-Murray, *Baptism in the New Testament*, p. 100.

Spirit (viii, 12–24). The laying on of hands marked the coming of the Spirit in Samaria (viii, 14–17) and Ephesus (xix, 5, 6) after baptism; or (as in Acts ix, 17, 18) before baptism.

(iii) The blessings of the new age which baptism makes real – forgiveness, entry into the Church, the fellowship of believers and that conquering new-born joy which is denoted by the word 'exultation' (Gr. *agalliasis*) and 'boldness of speech' (Gr. *parrhesia*)* – were offered by the Apostolic preaching as men 'heard the word' and 'believed'. It is a striking fact that, while the sequence of experiences in which the Spirit is involved is varied, the order of the initial events is clear and precise. Men hear the message of Christ; they exercise faith in Him; and then they confess their belief as they submit to baptism. And this complex of events is regarded as though all the separate parts took place simultaneously. We may cite Acts xviii, 8 as the most obvious witness to this fact: 'And many of the Corinthians hearing Paul believed and were baptized.'

This compressed statement explains why Paul can later appeal in his Epistles to baptism as marking the beginning of the Christian life; and why faith in Christ and the confession of Him in baptism were not treated as two separable acts. They belonged together in a period of Church history when, as soon as men and women came to faith in Christ, they sought baptism immediately. Acts viii, 35, 36 is positive evidence of this. James Denney has thus the right to comment: 'Baptism and faith are but the outside and the inside of the same thing.'†

The sequence of 'hearing', 'believing' and 'being baptized' is preserved throughout the book of Acts; and the frequency of mention gives an impressive continuity to the Apostolic practice. The cases are: ii, 37, 38; ii, 41; viii, 12, 13; viii, 35, 36; x, 44; xi, 14, 15; xvi, 14, 15; xvi, 32, 33; xviii, 8; xix, 5.

(iv) All in all, allowing for certain deviations from this regular pattern, the witness of Acts is straightforward. Baptism (with or without the laying on of hands – a practice recorded in Acts viii, 15–17, which some scholars describe as a rudimentary 'confirmation' of believers) is the rite of initia-

---

* These words are worth following up in a New Testament Wordbook, e.g. that by William Barclay or R. M. Pope (*Studies in the Language of St. Paul*, London, 1936).
† J. Denney, *The Death of Christ*, p. 185.

tion into the visible Church, if this term is allowable. It is administered to those who are addressed by the word of the Gospel and who respond (as the Methodist formulary has it) 'sincerely desiring to be saved from their sins by faith in Him'. Its mode follows that of the Jewish *tebilah* at proselyte baptism, namely, immersion (Acts viii, 38, 39). The Greek terms for 'baptize', 'baptism' mean strictly 'douse' or 'saturating'; and there is a lack of decisiveness as to the mode of baptism from the use of the language employed.

Recent studies, however, have paid more attention to the meanings which underlie the baptismal actions. While the thought of baptism = 'washing' from the defilements of sin is attested (e.g., 1 Corinthians vi, 11; Ephesians v, 26; Titus iii, 5 and possibly Revelation i, 5 (A.V.); viii, 14),* the more important emphasis for the theology of baptism falls on the idea of baptism = 'immersion in the sea of death' as typifying a death to the old life and a new creation, as J. Ysebaert phrases it.† The metaphor is linked with the removal of clothes before entering the baptismal bath, and the putting on of fresh garments upon the emergence from the water. Such a divestiture and re-clothing is often pictured in the thought of Paul (Galatians iii, 27; Colossians iii, 9 ff.) in a context of death and new life (cf. Romans xiii, 14; Colossians iii, 3 ff.); and the entire thought is related to Christ's death and baptism (Colossians ii, 11, 12; Ephesians iv, 21 ff.). The Pauline *locus classicus* for this line of teaching is Romans vi, 3 ff. to which we shall have occasion to refer; but that it is not peculiarly Paul's doctrine is clear from 1 Peter iii, 20 f. to iv, 1.

The households mentioned in regard to baptism in Acts are those of Lydia (xvi, 15) and the Philippian jailer (xvi, 33). The texts seem to pre-suppose that the entire 'families' (used in the wide sense to include servants and kinsmen) became committed to the faith. This fact seems evident as far as the latter case is concerned, for Acts xvi, 31–34 tells how the household is evangelized and entered, with the principal convert, into his joy. If this reading is correct – and the debate about infant baptism still continues among New Testament

* See too Hebrews x, 22; Acts xxii, 16: 'Rise and be baptized, and wash away your sins, calling on his name' (R.S.V.) is less certain; and it is arguable (with H. W. Robinson) that the participle 'calling upon his name' is the ground of the appeal 'wash away your sins' rather than the invitation to baptism.

† J. Ysebaert, *Greek Baptismal Terminology*, p. 53.

scholars and Church historians* – then the age of the members of the households is immaterial; the fact that they came into the fellowship of believers is all-important for the theology of Acts as a whole.

No countenance is given to any magical or superstitious notions of baptismal efficacy (see, by way of illustration, Acts viii, 13 and 21). Moreover, we should not fail to observe that baptism is never presented as an optional extra to Christian discipleship. It follows directly upon the initial act of faith, and may be said to be complementary to it. The call 'Why do you wait? Rise and be baptized' (Acts xxii, 16, R.S.V.) is the order that early Christians accepted with alacrity. Pre-baptismal instruction and the catechumenate came later – although some scholars find an allusion to the preparation of candidates in Hebrews vi, 2, and even traces of a baptismal service in 1 Peter and 1 John.† But some of the theories which have been proposed require a reading back from Church practice of a later century (notably the third century Church Order of Hippolytus) into the New Testament period – and this is a questionable procedure.

II. *St. Paul's Doctrine of Baptism*

Paul appears on the New Testament scene as 'a wise master-builder' (1 Corinthians iii, 10) who, under God, reared up the great edifice of Christian truth. But, as we have already had occasion to observe, he used stones 'already quarried and hewn into rough shape' (to use A. M. Hunter's phrase)‡ by his pre-decessors, by those who were 'in Christ' before him (Romans xvi, 7). This understanding of Paul's mission will be confirmed by our study of his teaching on baptism.

He was no inventor, but displayed in many ways a dependence upon the teaching which earlier Christian preachers had delivered to the members of the Churches to which he wrote (Romans vi, 17). Thus he can appeal to Christians in

* The latest contribution to the debate is that by J. Jeremias, *The Origins of Infant Baptism* (London, E. T., 1963).

† See on 1 Peter, F. L. Cross, *1 Peter – A Paschal Liturgy* (Oxford, 1954) and for an examination of his theory, the present writer's art. 'The Composition of 1 Peter in Recent Study', *Vox Evangelica i* (London, 1962), pp. 36 ff. For the view that 1 John contains liturgical material see W. Nauck, *Die Tradition und der Charakter des ersten Johannesbriefes* (Tübingen, 1957).

‡ A. M. Hunter, *Paul and his Predecessors* (London, 1961) p. 115.

the capital city of the Empire: 'Surely you know that . . .' (Romans vi, 3) – and this is his way of introducing an elaborate discussion on the significance of the ordinance of baptism. He assumes that baptism for them all without apparent exception will be a familiar Church practice and experience (so Romans vi, 3: 'all of us'); and the same assumption is made of the Colossians, whom he had never met (Colossians ii, 1). At least this fact is common to both writer and readers – that both had entered the gateway of the Christian faith and the fellowship of the Church by the initiatory rite of baptism (Colossians ii, 12; and for Paul himself, see Acts ix, 18; xx, 16).

The chief contribution of the Apostle was to enlarge the understanding of his converts and fellow-believers as to the deeper significance of what they already knew and experienced. This was his God-given task as 'a teacher of the Gentiles' (1 Timothy ii, 7). He assumes that baptism is 'in' or 'into' the name of Christ, and is a symbol of cleansing (1 Corinthians i, 13, vi, 11; Ephesians v, 26); and, as Acts also depicts the rite, the Pauline literature regards baptism as the outward sign of admittance into the fellowship of the Church. The positive and negative contributions of the Apostle, however, are made in terms of the drawing out of some latent implications, and the stating of some drastic basic truths in relation to an accepted Christian practice. Three points call for comment.

(i) First, and this is a negative consideration, yet of some considerable importance: Paul recoils from any superstitious use of the sacraments. The Corinthians imagined that to have been baptized by some important person (like Peter, Apollos, Paul himself) was an occasion of great benefit to them. And they had a strange practice of baptizing Church members for their deceased relatives and friends. Paul dissociates himself from the implied superstition of the first idea. There is no magical bond set up between the baptizer and his convert – a notion which was current in the pagan religious customs of his day (1 Corinthians i, 13–17). He neither favours nor condemns the latter practice. He simply uses it as an illustration. See 1 Corinthians xv, 29.

But his discussions of the meaning of baptism and the Lord's Supper in 1 Corinthians i, 16, 17 and x, 1–17 show that he taught no magical ideas, nor gave the impression that the sacraments conferred some special power. These ceremonial

acts, he is at pains to make clear, are no substitute for communion with the Lord and a disciplined turning aside from all
evil. They 'are no safeguard for a careless life which takes
liberties with itself' (in Moffatt's phrase).*

(ii) Two passages demonstrate the meaning of baptism as a
means of entry into the community of the Church, Christ's
body (1 Corinthians xii, 13; Galatians iii, 27). The conversion-
baptism experience introduced the believer into a universal
fellowship where there are no barriers of race (neither Jew
nor Greek), social condition (neither bond nor free) or sex
(neither male nor female). His membership of the body of
believers is regarded as nothing less than a membership of
Christ whom he 'put on' (Galatians iii, 27). With this latter
verse, we should compare Romans xiii, 14; Ephesians iv, 24;
Colossians iii, 10 which are sections of Paul's writings to
illustrate this 'putting on' as no mystical experience, but rather
one of the most practical and searchingly ethical kind. At baptism the new convert became an inheritor of the privileges and
responsibilities which were his as a partaker of Christ, an 'heir
acording to the promise'. He, like his Lord, receives the seal
of adoption (Galatians iv, 1–7), and is called to 'live out' the
risen life of Christ (Galatians iv, 19).

(iii) This clarion call to live as those who are dead to self
and alive to God is sounded in Romans vi, 1–4 in a baptismal
context. St. Paul's ethical motives and standards are not – contrary to some popular conceptions – in terms of 'Follow Jesus
and do your best', but in terms of death and the new life
which stems from union with the risen Lord (see 1 Corinthians vi, 17 for a classic definition of this union).

Baptism clearly means this in this total picture of the
Christian man,† as the snatch of baptismal hymnody in
Ephesians v, 14 makes plain. The convert is plunged into the
water – this means a dying with Christ. He remains there for
a moment under the surface – this means that he is buried with
Him. He emerges from the water – this means that he is being
raised with Him. Christian opinion is divided over the meaning of Paul's teaching in this striking, if difficult, passage. Is the
Apostle using baptism as a simple and symbolic illustration

* J. Moffatt, *The First Epistle of Paul to the Corinthians* (London,
1938), p. 129.

† The classic paraphrase of the baptismal instruction in Romans vi
is in Sanday and Headlam's commentary, International Critical Commentary on the Epistle (Edinburgh, 1902), p. 154.

of what happens spiritually when a man is converted? If so, his language is involved and needlessly realistic.

At the other extreme, some scholars have said that Paul is borrowing from the Greek Mystery religions which believed that baptism by its simple performance – and sometimes connected with the sacrifice of an animal whose blood was poured over the initiate – automatically led to the 'rebirth' of the devotee who became quite literally, in the eyes of the religion, a new creature. But the analogies which used to be drawn from these Hellenistic sources have been critically scrutinized in an authoritative, recent work by G. Wagner and shown to be wanting.* For Paul, it is the *moral* emphases of baptism which are vital; and the only rebirth which engages his interest is that which makes a man alive to God in the realm of moral consciousness and endeavour (Romans vi, 6–11). A more likely view of the chapter is that Paul's language is to be taken literally, yet interpreted in a dynamic sense. The best analogy is that of the symbolic actions of the Old Testament prophets. The resultant picture is somewhat as follows.

Paul is describing here what really happens in baptism which (in the early Church) followed so closely upon conversion that the two experiences could be spoken of in the same breath and as virtual synonyms. Baptism is no empty symbol or 'bare sign', but a genuine sacramental action in which God works, applies the saving efficacy of the death and resurrection of Christ in which we died and rose again, and places us in that sphere of divine life in which sin is conquered (Romans vi, 7, 9–11). Henceforth, the Christian is called to become in his daily living what he already is 'in Christ',† to work out the implications of what his baptism meant (verses 12 ff.), as the circumcised Israelite needed to 'make good' his circumcision by a life of obedience within the covenant (Colossians ii, 9–13; cf. Romans ii, 25–29; 1 Corinthians vii, 18 f.). This means that baptism is invalid, because meaningless, where there is no faith.‡

* G. Wagner, *Das religionsgeschichtliche Problem von Römer 6, 1–11* (Zürich, 1962).

† C. H. Dodd (*The Epistle of Paul to the Romans:* London, 1932) writes on this passage: 'The maxim all through is: "Become what you are." The Christian is a member of Christ: he must see to it that in the empirical life of moral endeavour he becomes more and more that which a member of Christ should be.'

‡ Most would agree here, but the relation between baptism and faith is a matter of acute disagreement in the modern debate. Paedobaptists

E. F. Scott comments on Ephesians v, 25–27 (in which 'with the word' implies some formula of confession): 'The ceremony itself meant nothing apart from the "word" or confession which gave expression to a vital faith.'* And the story of Philip (Acts viii, 36 ff.) shows how much importance was placed on a declaration of personal commitment.

In summary, there are two sides to Paul's baptismal teaching as we glean it from the texts above. 1 Corinthians vii, 14c is generally now agreed to be immaterial in this discussion.† The ordinance 're-presents' the saving acts and events of the Gospel, portraying in a dramatic way the death and rising of Jesus. And in so far as conversion and baptism are two sides of the same coin, the sacrament brings to the participant the reality it signifies. But this is done not in any mechanical fashion, as though the mere performance of the rite guaranteed its inevitable efficacy. Always the subjective side is needed. What God has done (in the Gospel) and does (in the baptism) requires a personal appropriation; and this means, on the human side, the indispensability of faith (so exactly Colossians ii, 12, as well as the general principle set out in Ephesians ii, 8).

III. *Some Aspects of New Testament Baptism*

The whole subject of the New Testament doctrine of Christian initiation is much to the fore in recent scholarship; and bristles with so many difficulties of interpretation that widely divergent views are possible. It is not the purpose of these chapters to

* E. F. Scott, *The Epistles to the Colossians, to Philemon and to the Ephesians* (London, 1930), p. 240.
† G. R. Beasley-Murray, op. cit., pp. 192 ff., surveys the past debate and concludes: 'It (1 Corinthians vii, 14) would be best omitted from the discussion concerning (the) doctrine' (p. 199). See for the most recent pronouncement J. Jeremias, *The Origins of Infant Baptism* (London, E. T. 1963), p. 37.

construe the necessity of faith in terms of the proleptic anticipation of the response which the child will make when he is grown, or else in terms of the faith of the Church into which the child is baptized. Tied with the first idea is the conviction that the Cross was a general, all-inclusive and prevenient baptism which antedates all human response: see J. A. T. Robinson, art. 'The one Baptism' in *Twelve New Testament Studies* (London, 1962).

O. Cullmann's chapter in *Baptism in the New Testament* and G. R. Beasley-Murray's section, op. cit., both headed 'Baptism and Faith' show the extent of the disagreement.

canvass the modern debate, let alone pronounce upon the correctness and error of influential theories. Our task is more modest. It is simply – if this aim is at all possible – to extract the minimum of agreed content from the New Testament documents of what constituted the early Christian baptismal teaching and practice within the context of the worshipping life of the Church.

Some general picture of St. Paul's contribution has just been drawn. May this be further clarified by our considering the remaining New Testament books – or does the overall impression require some modification in the light of what we have still to discuss? It will perhaps be helpful if we state the New Testament estimate in some broad terms, drawn from Paul's writings, and then add in the witness of the other literature.

(i) The fullest exposition of the inner meaning of the outward actions of baptism is to be found in Romans vi, 3 ff. and Colossians ii, 12; and both texts set the sacramental significance firmly within the context of death and resurrection. The later witness of Titus iii, 5 agrees with this emphasis: 'He saved us through the bath of rebirth and renewing of the Holy Spirit.'* Here the new birth of the Christian as a child of God is traced to the working of the Holy Spirit who uses the instrumental means of baptism to bring to the newly awakened person the knowledge of his life in Christ. The words of John iii, 5; 'born from water and the Spirit' say the same thing, and this thought is enlarged in 1 John v, 8 possibly, in the phrase 'the Spirit, the water, and the blood', to include and cover the chief parts of initiation into the Church's life through the rites of baptism and the Communion.†

C. F. D. Moule has called attention to the New Testament stress on baptism as 'essentially *death* and *burial* – not mere *washing*.'‡ This latter metaphor is found, as at 1 Corinthians vi, 11 and Ephesians v, 26, but the characteristic note is sounded in the call which the ceremony issues to death to sin and self, and rising to newness of Christ's risen life. 1 Peter repeats this theme by treating its readers as 'new-born babes'

* Other references in the Pastorals may be quoted here: e.g., the baptismal hymn of 2 Timothy ii, 11–13 on which cf. the comments and bibliography in *Vox Evangelica ii* (London, 1963), p. 20.

† So W. Nauck, op. cit., excursus I and T. W. Manson, art. 'Entry into Membership of the Early Church' *Journal of Theological Studies*, xlviii, 1947, pp. 25 ff.

‡ C. F. D. Moule, *Worship in the New Testament*, p. 57.

whose sinful past has been drowned in the water of baptism, even as the wicked generation of Noah's times perished in the Flood (1 Peter iii, 20 ff.).

It is interesting that Paul links preparation for baptism in stripping off the baptizand's clothes and the subsequent investiture of new clothing with the putting off of the old nature and the putting on of the new. In those sections of Ephesians and Colossians which speak of the Christians life as a death to the past life and a rising to newness of ethical behaviour, baptism is pictured as marking the transition and change (see Colossians ii, 12; iii, 1 in the total context of i, 11: 'putting off the body of the sins of the flesh . . .' iii, 5: 'Put to death . . .' iii, 8: 'Put off the old habits . . .' iii, 10: 'Put on the new man'; iii, 12: 'Put on the new virtues').

Galatians iii, 27 sums up the Pauline thought with conciseness: 'Baptized into union with him, you have all put on Christ as a garment.' The thought of disrobing for immersion and the subsequent reclothing with new garments are facts which enable the Apostle to draw out the deep meaning of the rite: the candidate in that act is called upon to renounce his old way of life, shedding it as an old garment; and then, to accept the challenge of a new life, as though he were putting on a brand new set of clothes which befits his new status in the family of God (Galatians vi, 15; 2 Corinthians v, 17).

(ii) Confession of Christ at baptism, which seems to have been a regular feature in Acts and the Pauline teaching (for instance Romans x, 9, 10), may also explain the words of 1 Peter iii, 21 in which an enigmatic term (translated by 'the *answer* of a good conscience') may be the equivalent of the Latin *stipulatio* and stand for the idea of baptism as a seal of contract between the convert and God. His baptismal profession of faith is then the thought in view; and answers to the 'word of faith' of Romans x. 8.

(iii) We have already noticed how the new life in Christ is likened to a resurrection and an awakening from the dead. Not far away from this notion is the imagery of light. The believer is brought out of darkness (of ignorance, unbelief, evil practices) into the marvellous light of the Gospel hope (1 Peter ii, 11). It is only natural, therefore, that baptism should be described in the later Church as 'enlightenment' (as in Justin Martyr in the second century). And it may be that this usage goes back to Hebrews vi, 4; x, 32. Clearly Ephesians v, 14 may be regarded as a baptismal invocation:

'Awake, O sleeper,
From thy grave arise.
The light of Christ upon thee shines.'

(iv) There are parts of the New Testament Scripture where we may plausibly seek not only mention of the act of baptism, but of a series of acts associated with Church membership.* Admittedly this means reading back from a later time when such ceremonials were common practice. The ceremonials are: anointing with oil (cf. 1 John ii, 20 ff.), which is sometimes alluded to as 'sealing' (see 2 Corinthians i, 22; Ephesians 1, 13; iv, 30; 2 Timothy ii, 19); the laying on of hands (with special application to ordination: the hymns of 1 Timothy vi, 11–16; 2 Timothy ii, 11–13 may refer to this); and the tasting of new food (in the first Communion administered following baptism. Some scholars find allusion to this in Hebrews vi 4 f. and 1 Peter ii, 3). Post-baptismal lustrations may too be referred to in Hebrews vi, 2; x, 22 and John xiii, 10.†

It is easy to be incautious about some of these identifications and to be attracted by a superficial resemblance of language only. The danger of a 'pan-liturgism' (that is, the temptation to see early Christian worship in almost every place of the New Testament writings and to treat it as the key to open every lock of exegetical difficulty) is a present one today; and we do well to heed the salutary warning of Professor van Unnik‡ who reminds us that the liturgies and Church orders are *later in time* than the literature of the pristine Church of the first century. What we may learn positively, however, from the verses referred to above is that baptism was no solitary rite of initiation into the Church, but part undoubtedly of a wider complex of actions and experiences by which a person was led, with opened eyes, 'from darkness to light, and from the power of Satan unto God' to the receiving of 'forgiveness of sins, and inheritance among them who are sanctified by faith' in Jesus Christ (Acts xxvi, 18).

* The Gospel of John has been subjected to some investigation with a view to exposing an alleged sacramentalism in its narratives and discourses; see especially O. Cullmann, *Early Christian Worship*, pp. 37 ff.

† Or conceivably these texts relate to baptism itself: see the lucid discussions in *Christian Baptism* (ed. A. Gilmore), chap. 4.

‡ W. C. van Unnik, art. '*Dominus Vobiscum:* The Background of a Liturgical Formula', *New Testament Essays in Memory of T. W. Manson* (ed. A. J. B. Higgins: Manchester, 1959), p. 272.

10

The Supper in the Upper Room –
Its Background and Significance

No event in the last days of the Lord's earthly ministry has fastened itself more securely upon the Christian imagination than what took place, in the Thursday of Holy Week, in the guest-chamber of one of His nameless friends in Jerusalem. He gathered His followers around Him in sacred association as they shared together the traditional Passover meal. The Gospel writers do not answer all our questions concerning the precise nature and import of this meal; and hence these matters are the topics for a lively and continuing debate.* What does seem clear is that, for the Synoptic evangelists of the first three Gospels, the last Supper is firmly set within the framework of the Paschal feast. If we take this fact as our starting point, it will help us to see the setting of the meal and give us a window into the mind of Jesus and His disciples on 'the night when He was betrayed'.

(I) *Preparing the Passover*

In Exodus xii, Moses is reported as coming to the elders of Israel with instructions given to him by God for the observance of a feast that was to accompany the nation's liberation from Egyptian bondage.† But this festival was to have a significance far beyond the historical situation in which it was born. When the Israelite people came into the land of Canaan and were established as the people of God in the land of

* Possibly the most useful survey of the New Testament teaching is that by A. J. B. Higgins, *The Lord's Supper in the New Testament* (London, 1952). A more recent attempt to cover the ground is by Paul Neuenzeit, *Das Herrenmahl* (München, 1960); and the present writer has contributed to the N.B.D. under 'Lord's Supper', pp. 748–52.

† For a comprehensive history of the Passover, see J. B. Segal, *The Hebrew Passover* (Oxford, 1963).

promise, this festival was to be kept every year as 'an ordinance to thee and to thy sons for ever' (Exodus xii, 24). The Passover was given a setting in the life of the nation which was to be as permanent as the life of the nation itself (Exodus xii, 14, 17). It cannot therefore be without significance that, in the ministry of Jesus, whose mission as the Elect One (Luke ix, 35; xxiii, 35: both texts speak of Him as God's Chosen) recapitulated so much of Israel's life, history and destiny, His public career moves inexorably to His Passion and sacrifice at the Passover season. The first three Gospels make this fact very plain with their historical notices:

> 'Now the first day of the feast of unleavened bread the disciples came to Jesus, saying unto him, Where wilt thou that we prepare for thee to eat the passover?'
>
> (Matthew xxvi, 17).

> 'And the first day of unleavened bread, when they killed the passover, his disciples saith unto him . . .'
>
> (Mark xiv, 12).

> 'Then came the day of unleavened bread when the passover must be killed'
>
> (Luke xxii, 7).

The Lord Jesus, in full recognition that His hour had come, bids His disciples to make ready the Paschal feast; and this preparation will be the first step along the *via dolorosa* which will at length bring Him to Gethsemane, Gabbatha and Golgotha.

In the Synoptic tradition, the meal is set in the 'large upper room' in the city of Jerusalem (Luke xxii, 12, 13); and is apparently described as the regular Passover feast. But certain difficulties are present when we place alongside this evidence the teaching of John's Gospel, according to which Jesus died at the same time as the Passover lambs were being immolated in the Temple ritual (see John xiii, 1; xviii, 28; xix, 14, 31, 42 as the texts which imply that on the day we know as Good Friday the Passover for the Jewish leaders was still future). Added to this is the view which some scholars hold that Luke xxii, 15, 16 records an unfulfilled wish on the part of the Lord. On this understanding of the text (and there is some doubt as to the actual reading to be preferred in the Greek), the sense of the verses is conveyed in F. C. Burkitt's paraphrase: 'Near as this Passover is, and much as I have longed to celebrate it with you, it is not so to be; for I shall not eat it; within the next twenty-four hours the enemy will have done his worst, and the next Passover I shall eat with you will be the Messianic feast.'* The account which follows sets the meal in a Passover mould, although it was not (on this view) the regular Passover feast.

A number of ingenious solutions to this complex problem of the exact identification of the last meal in the Upper Room have been offered, and may be read about elsewhere.† The latest writer on the subject confesses that no final solution has yet been made, and the matter should be left open.‡

But we should be aware that, of recent years, some scholars have come back to the plain witness of the Synoptics that the meal in the Upper Room has all the features of the Passover celebration. A New Testament authority on matters of the Jewish background of the Gospels, Professor Jeremias has shown how there are eleven items in the records which point to the Paschal setting of the meal.§ It took place in the holy city; it was held at night-time; it brought together a small band of men, thus preserving the 'domestic' atmosphere of the Jewish family feast; the disciples reclined at table – a peculiarity to which the children of Jewish households today draw attention by a question; a dish preceded the breaking of the bread; red wine was drunk – a special Passover feature; almsgiving was associated with this feast (cf. John xiii, 29); the meal closed with the Hallel-hymn drawn from Psalms cxiii–cxviii; the Lord's words over the bread and the wine find a natural place as a piece of Scriptural exposition which was common at Passover; the use of a 'sop' (John xiii, 26 f.) is an evidence of the nature of the meal, for this sop (a piece of bread dipped in a specially prepared sauce as a memorial of bitterness of the Egyptian bondage) belongs to the annual feast (see Mark xiv, 20); and so on.

But there are contrary points to be reckoned with. In an earlier chapter we drew attention to the absence of the lamb from the Lord's meal-table, and noted that some recent writers

* See *Journal of Theological Studies*, ix, 1908, pp. 569–72.

† N.B.D., pp. 748–49.

‡ A. Gilmore, art. 'The Date and Significance of the Last Supper', *Scottish Journal of Theology*, 14 Sept., 1961, p. 269.

§ J. Jeremias, *The Eucharistic Words of Jesus* (Oxford, E.T., 1955) pp. 14 ff. and for a convenient summary, his article, 'The Last Supper', *Journal of Theological Studies*, 1, 1949, pp. 1–10 may be consulted.

have sought to explain this omission in different ways.* Of course, it may be that the Passover lamb was left out for the simple reason that the true Lamb of God (John i, 29) was Himself present and would shortly offer Himself for the greater redemption of His people and the world (see this thought in John xix, 29, 36; 1 Corinthians v, 6–8; 1 Peter i, 18, 79; Revelation v, 6 ff., xiii, 8).†

Another objection to the simple equation, Last Supper equals the Passover feast, arises from the witness of John's Gospel. But, in spite of certain chronological difficulties, it seems fairly clear that John xiii describes some features of the meal which betray its setting as a Passover festival. The sop and the almsgiving are but two of a number of such traits. An attempt has been made to overcome this divergence within the Fourth Gospel itself by suggesting that our Lord followed one calendar and held the meal on 14 Nisan, whereas the Pharisees (who evidently have still to eat the Passover in John xviii, 28) followed a different calendar. Evidence for the existence of separate festal calendars within Judaism has been supplied by the documents of the Dead Sea scrolls, so this theory is not pure speculation. But certain problems still remain unresolved.‡

At all events, whether the Lord's last meal with the disciples was the regular Passover, or an 'anticipated Passover' (as some scholars like Vincent Taylor think.§), or a meal such as Jewish 'friends' enjoyed as fellow-religionists and similar to those meals which He and the disciples shared in the course of the Galilean ministry (Mark ii, 13–17; vi, 39–44; viii, 6–8), it does seem clear that Paschal ideas were in His mind as He sat down with the Twelve.‖ The early Church looked back to this meal and its symbolism as portraying Him as the true Passover (1 Corinthians v, 7, 8); and Christian devotion has expressed it thus:

* See chap. 2, pp. 20 f.

† This note is sounded throughout the Gospel of John; cf. R. H. Lightfoot's commentary, *St. John's Gospel* (Oxford, 1956). Appended Note: The Lord the true Passover Feast, pp. 349 ff.

‡ See Jeremias' review of A. Jaubert's thesis in *Journal of Theological Studies* n.s. x, 1959, 131 ff.

§ V. Taylor, *The Gospel According to St. Mark* (London, 1952), pp. 665 f.

‖ There is a clear and important statement of this possibility in Théo Preiss, *Life in Christ* (London, E.T., 1954), pp. 81 ff. His essay is worthy of careful attention.

'Thou very Paschal Lamb,
Whose blood for us was shed,
Through whom we out of Egypt came,
Thy ransomed people lead.'

II. *Observing the Passover*   *A reliving & reenacting*
A reliving

The Jews' festival of national deliverance has a two-way look.
It bids the worshipper recall the Lord's mercy to His people
in the land of enslavement; and it points him to the Messianic
Age, when God's purposes for Israel will be fulfilled. But
both these thoughts, which might easily become vague generali-
ties, are given at Passover a special precision. It is not enough
that the family at the Paschal table remember the past redemption; they must relive it in a most realistic sense. And this
realism is carried over into the future hope of a national re-
lease from bondage and a restoration to the ancestral land. For
these reasons, the various dishes are invested with symbolic
meaning.* The bitter herbs forcefully remind the eaters
of the bitterness of the bondage their fathers suffered; the cups
are taken in token of a coming deliverance and salvation.

In a most important rubric the Rabbis laid it down that: 'in
every generation a man must so regard himself as if came
forth himself out of Egypt', quoting in support of this statement Exodus xiii, 8 and Deuteronomy vi, 20–23.† It is hard
to exaggerate the importance of these Biblical texts for the
Jewish understanding of the Passover. Each member of the
family was to regard himself as though he had been personally
in bondage in Egypt and had been personally brought out by
the Lord his God. Two parts of the Passover Liturgy
illustrates this.

The head of the household holds in his hand a loaf and
recites a formula which is drawn from Deuteronomy xvi, 3:
'This is the bread of affliction which our fathers ate when
they came out of Egypt.'‡ In the literal sense, of course, the
bread on the table of Jewish homes – and in the Upper Room
in Jerusalem at Jesus' last meal – is not the bread which
Moses took centuries before; but there *is* some relation between the two pieces of bread, for by the one which is held

* For symbolic values attaching to the Passover dishes, see Lev
Gillet, *Communion in the Messiah* (London, 1942). pp. 130, 131.
† The Mishnah, tractate *Pesachim* x, 5 (Danby's translation p. 151).
‡ See Higgins, op. cit., p. 53.

in the hand and eaten today the Jew is linked with the life of his nation and is taken back in a most vivid, realistic – and almost mystical – way to consider 'the rock whence ye were hewn and . . . the hole of the pit whence ye were digged' (Isaiah li, 1); and to share today in the redemption which the Lord wrought for His people long ago.

The second part of the Passover ritual which is meant to join past and present, is the telling of the story of the Exodus. This is known as the *Haggadah*, a word which means 'declaration' and is taken from the Hebrew of Exodus xiii, 8: 'And you *shall tell* your son on that day, "It is because of what the Lord did for me when I came out of Egypt".' This retelling of the story is a vital part of the Passover. 'Now even though all of us were wise . . . of great understanding . . . learned as elders . . . familiar with the Scripture, it would still be our duty to tell again the story of the Exodus' – so runs the Jewish regulation for the service.*

We have concentrated upon these points of the traditional Jewish Pascha because it is just at these points that we may enter into an understanding of the Upper Room meal and the Lord's Supper in the Christian Church of the Apostolic age – and this is the limit of our task, without trespassing into the subsequent development of the doctrine of the Eucharist in the later centuries.

The disciples, as faithful sons of ancient Israel, gathered in the room 'in remembrance of the departure from Egypt' (as the Jewish formula reads)† and in expectation that God would remember His covenant with Israel and send them national deliverance. All Jews believe that, as their nation had been set free on the first Passover, so God will send redemption on a future Paschal night. The token of this hope is the setting of a vacant place for Elijah who will come, it is believed, on Passover night as Messiah's herald.

With gratitude for God's past mercies to the people of which they formed a part, and with eager hope that His purposes for the restoring the Kingdom to Israel (Acts i, 6) would be ful-

* Quoted by and discussed by W. D. Davies, *Paul and Rabbinic Judaism* (London, 1955), p. 252.

* See W. D. Davies, op. cit., pp. 252 note 3; and J. J. Petuchowski, art. 'Do This in Remembrance of Me', *Journal of Biblical Literature* lxxvi, 1957, pp. 293 ff.

filled, the disciples sat down on that never-to-be-forgotten occasion of the night in which He was betrayed.

III. *Interpreting the Passover*

Although there had been many precedents for a meal between Jesus and His own followers in the course of the Galilean ministry, this meal was unique. The Lord's own attitude to it is revealed in His words of Luke xxii, 15: 'How I have longed to eat this Passover with you before my death!' (N.E.B.). The special significance of this Passover which stamped it with an unforgettable importance which St. Paul referred to years later (1 Corinthians xi, 23) was not in what He did, but *in what He said*. At certain places in the customary service He interjected His words of interpretation, and thereby illumined three topics.

(i) *The words of institution* (Matthew xxvi, 26 ff.; Mark xiv, 22 ff.; Luke xxii, 19 ff.).

With the bread before Him and them on the table, the disciples heard Him say, 'This is my body which is given for you'; and after the meal, over a closing cup of wine, 'This cup is the new covenant in my blood.' If we recall that Jesus spoke Aramaic, we shall not attach any literal significance to the verb in the English translation, 'is', for the verb 'to be' was omitted in the spoken language and the meaning left to be inferred (see Genesis xl, 12; Daniel ii, 36 for examples drawn from the Old Testament).* He said, 'This bread – my body.' Moffatt tries to bring out the sense by translating 'means', and this rendering is supported by the use of the verb 'to be' in Galatians iv, 24. 'These women *represent* two covenants' must be the sense of the A.V.: 'These *are* the two covenants.'

The key, however, to His words lies in the Passover interpretation of Deuteronomy xvi, 3. While the Jews say that the bread and the wine in the various Paschal cups stand for the past redemption which is thereby brought into the present and made to relive, Jesus declared that the bread in His hands stands for His body, shortly to be yielded up in the service of

---

* A slightly fuller discussion of 'transubstantiation' in the light of the Last Supper verses is given in the author's booklet, *The Lord's Supper* (Crusade publication, 1960), pp. 7 f.; and I have borrowed some sentences from this publication in the text above.

God's redeeming purpose (Hebrews x, 5–10); and His blood, outpoured in death, recalling the sacrificial rites of the Old Testament, is represented in the cup of blessing on the table. Both dishes are invested with a new significance – a parabolic one – as they speak of (and bring into the present for personal appropriation by the Church, as often as the Lord's Table is spread) the new Exodus which He effected for His people. Of this meaning of His death the New Testament speaks in Luke ix, 31: 'the *exodus*, the destiny He was to fulfil at Jerusalem'.

(ii) *The new covenant*

The cup is associated with the covenant (Exodus xxiv, 3–11) which God made with the nation of Israel. But this compact was a failure because of Israel's defection (Jeremiah iii, 20; xxxi, 32) and rebellion (Isaiah i, 2; Hosea vi, 7 f.). Jeremiah speaks, therefore, of a new covenant which the Lord will make Jeremiah xxxi, 31–34); and the fulfilment of this hope is announced in the Upper Room, with the emphasis falling on those elements which Jeremiah had predicted: the inwardness of faith, personal responsibility, and the pledge of a full forgiveness. No animal sacrifice could secure this (for the Law made nothing perfect, Hebrews vii, 19); the blood of God's own One was needed – and was offered – for this consummate purpose (Acts xx, 28).

It is not unexpected that Jesus, with His eye on His impending death, will speak of that death as the drinking of a cup (Mark x, 38, 39). The symbol of a cup had long been part of the Old Testament vocabulary to express man's relationship to God. Under the Divine blessing, his life is a happy one, with a cup filled with joy (Psalm xvi, 5; xxiii, 5). If a man rebels and chooses his own way, he receives the condign judgement of a bitter cup (Psalm xi, 6; Ezekiel xxiii, 33; Psalm lxxv, 8). Thus, the cup becomes in this context a symbol of the wrath and condemnation of God (see Isaiah li, 17 for this appalling metaphor). Yet this is not the only meaning, and the Psalmist can go on to celebrate the goodness of God with a cup of thanksgiving (Psalm cxvi, 13); and the sharing of a common cup denotes the greatest intimacy (2 Samuel xii, 3 for a touching reference to this!).

With so many nuances to be understood from the use of the cup, it is not possible to say exactly what was in the Lord's mind as He pointed to red wine on the Passover table and exclaimed, 'This cup means My covenant-blood'. Certainly, we should see in this allusion an interpretation of His death as inaugurating the new covenant of Jeremiah with the overtone that this new covenant will only be ratified as He accepts from the Father's hand 'the cup which our sins had mingled'* and tastes the bitter experience of sin-bearing and separation from God on the Cross. But while His work is solitary and unique, He calls His followers to share the benefits and avail themselves of the fruits of His Passion; for in drinking the cup (as in eating the bread) they will be appropriating His life laid down in sacrifice and taken up in newness of power. John vi, 32 ff. preserves this teaching that His work does not avail unless it is received, even as food does not nourish until it is assimilated and made part of our very life. His atonement *for us* (*extra nos*) must be complemented by His work *in us* (*in nobis*) – so 'He that eateth my flesh, and drinketh my blood, dwelleth in me, and I in him' (John vi, 56). And a somewhat similar strand of teaching is found in 1 Corinthians x, 16. Both the cup and bread are the means of sharing in the blood and the body that were offered for our redemption.

(iii) *The command to repeat*

Because Jesus attached this significance to His death and its parabolic enactment in the bread and the cup, it is natural that He should go on to speak about a command for His actions at the table to be perpetuated. Luke xxii, 19 (A.V.) contains the words: 'This do in remembrance of me', an instruction renewed in Paul's account of 1 Corinthians xi, 24, 25. Possibly no other single Scriptural sentence has occasioned so much controversy and bad blood between Christians as this one; and acrimonious debate finds here its storm-centre. To dispel the difficulty of Eucharistic controversy in a few words may be presumptuously foolhardy, but if the key is found in the Passover vocabulary, much light is shed on this text. The Hebrew Pascha was instituted 'for a memorial' (Exodus xii, 14; xiii, 9); and (as we observed earlier) by this 'sacramental' means the nation is carried back to, and caught up into, God's redeeming action. Likewise, at the Table of remembrance, the Church does not simply reflect (as a mental exercise) upon the Cross of Calvary, but relives the accom-

* James Denney's phrase.

plished redemption, is taken back to the Upper Room and the Hill, shares in that saving work which it knows as a present reality – because its Author is the living One in the midst of His ransomed people.* And this present consciousness of the living Christ at His Table is a foretaste of and prelude to a richer fellowship in His Kingdom; for in the Upper Room He added to 'Adieu' the note of 'Au revoir' in His promise that His people would gather at His table in the final Kingdom (Matthew xxvi, 29; Mark xiv, 25; Luke xxii, 29, 30; John vi, 54).

* In this sense, we may approve the phrase 'the real Presence' (cf. Matthew xviii, 20; Revelation i, 17, 18; iii, 20).

11

The Lord's Supper in the Early Church

It is true to say that the doctrine of the Lord's Supper in the New Testament is distinctively Pauline doctrine. This evaluation does not mean that none of the other Apostolic writers mentions it or implies it; nor does it mean that St. Paul is a 'sacramentalist' – in the modern, opprobrious sense of the term! The fact is that the Apostle was (providentially, we may believe) faced at Corinth with a situation which required a careful statement of the Eucharistic teaching; and it was the exigency of the trouble within the Corinthians' assembly where the practice of the Lord's Table was misunderstood which called forth his extended writing on the subject. It is a possibility (so James Moffatt believes*) that 'had it not been for some irreverent behaviour at Corinth, we might never have known what he believed about the Lord's Supper'. Certainly, as a statistical fact, little is said about the Church's fellowship meal in the other Pauline Letters.

The chief part of the New Testament apart from the Pauline writings which is important – excluding of course the Synoptic narratives of the Last Supper which in turn may be thought to reflect the practice of the early communities – lies in Jesus' discourse on the bread of life in John vi, 1–14, 26–71. It is a matter of some dispute whether the imagery of eating the flesh and drinking the blood of the Son of man refers to the Communion. Many Christians hold this to be the case, and many Communion prayers and service-books are based on the idea of 'feeding on Him in our hearts with thanksgiving'. Whether this is legitimate or not, it is certainly a thought that must have repulsed the Jews, who knew that to drink the blood of a beast was abhorrent (Leviticus xvii, 10 ff.; 1 Samuel xiv, 34). It is more likely that the strong language of

* J. Moffatt, *Grace in the New Testament* (London, 1931), p. 157.

the Lord's discourse is aimed at those who denied a real incarnation – known as the Docetics; for the word 'body' (in the Synoptic verses, 'This is my body') has been changed into 'my flesh' (as in John i, 14 and 1 John iv, 2 f., 2 John 7). The interesting thing is that it is another writer belonging to what F. Loofs has called the 'Asia Minor tradition'* – Ignatius of Antioch – who both opposed the Docetic heresy of his day and carried forward the teaching of the Lord's Supper as a meal which had immortalizing properties (Ephesians xx, 2).† Moreover, Ignatius, in this chapter, uses the same title as in John vi: the Son of man; and it is the sole occurrence of this title in the Apostolic Fathers of the second century.

Other New Testament references to the Eucharist are traced in Hebrews vi, 4; xiii, 10; 1 Peter ii, 3; 2 Peter ii, 13; Jude 12 – but some of these allusions are very doubtful. All in all, we are dependent on St. Paul's teaching for our knowledge of the doctrine, and that teaching is contained for the most part within one Letter – the first Corinthian epistle.

Paul's Doctrine of the Lord's Supper‡

In this subject (as we noted earlier in regard to baptism) Paul was no innovator, introducing a teaching which his contemporaries suspected as newfangled and foreign to the Gospel which they had known. The idea that Paul was such a novel teacher was a cherished notion of theologians in the early part of the present century. But the evidence is against it, and the theory that the Apostle was a Hellenist who foisted on the Church a sacramental doctrine which was modelled on the Greek Mystery practice of a meal in honour of a cult deity is rightly discredited. The one important piece of evidence for this theory was the description given in the Acts of the Apostles of the 'breaking of bread' (Acts ii, 42, 46; xx, 7) without reference to the cup and the atoning death of Jesus. It was believed that Paul introduced these elements as startling innovations (1 Corinthians xi, 23 ff.).

But this elaborate theory is unnecessary. The non-mention

---

* F. Loofs, *Leitfaden der Dogmengeschichte*[4] i, (Tübingen, 1906), p. 100.
† Ignatius writes: 'Jesus Christ, who was of the family of David according to the flesh, the Son of Man and the Son of God, so that you obey the bishop and the presbytery with an undisturbed mind, breaking bread, which is the medicine of immortality, the antidote that we should not die, but live for ever in Jesus Christ.'
‡ See N.B.D. 'Lord's Supper', pp. 750 f.

of the cup may not be significant. The name 'breaking of bread' may be a sort of technical term for the whole meal, a *pars pro toto*. The grain of truth in the reconstruction which placed a dichotomy between the simple, non-sacramental meal in Acts and the later, elaborate cult-festival in honour of a dying and rising God – a theory of Pauline innovation associated with the name of Hans Lietzmann* – is that at Corinth the believers had tended to observe the Lord's Table with more emphasis on the ecstatic joy which characterized the post-resurrection meals† than upon the inner meaning of the rite as setting forth the death of the Lord Jesus in solemn fashion. Paul found it needful to remind them of this, but he does so in a way that does not suggest the introducing a new line of instruction. He is recalling the Church to what is traditional teaching (1 Corinthians xi, 23).

Besides, the clearest proof we have of Paul's faithful exposition of the doctrine in keeping with the Apostolic heritage into which he entered is the way in which he unfolds all that is implicit in the Lord's own teaching in the Upper Room.‡ Three features marked this dominical teaching, as we noted:

(i) There was a common meal and table-fellowship;

(ii) As bread and wine were taken, the Lord's presence was to be recalled 'in remembrance of Me';

(iii) The simple rite pointed beyond itself to a future hope in the Kingdom of God.

Paul's contribution lies in an application of these basic ideas.

(i) Nothing is more characteristic of the Apostle's sacramental teaching as a whole than his use of the term 'fellowship' (Gr. *koinonia*).§ In baptism we are united with Christ in His death and risen life; in the Lord's Supper we share in His body and blood. This is the plain sense of 1 Corinthians x, 16. By a receiving of the bread and wine and in response to faith – for the elements have no inherent efficacy or magical power to produce the blessing they signify – the believer is united to the sacrifice of Christ. Paul seems to have in view

* H. Lietzmann, *Mass and Lord's Supper* (Leiden, E.T. 1953 f.). For an excellent critique, see A. J. B. Higgins's article in *The Expository Times*, lxv, 11, 1954, pp. 333–36; also recently W. Rordorf, *Der Sonntag* (Zürich, 1962), pp. 219 ff.

† Luke xxiv, 30–35; John xxi, 9 ff.; Acts i, 4, R.V. marg., x, 41.

‡ See A. M. Hunter, *Paul and his Predecessors*, pp. 75 ff., 139.

§ See N.B.D., art. 'Communion', p. 245 f. for a discussion by the present writer of this New Testament key-term.

the purpose of the bread and wine as signifying to the Christian what the Passover dishes mean to the Jew. As we have seen, we are to understand the latter as the means by which the Jew is taken back in dynamic fashion and made to relive the experience of his forbears in the land of Egypt. By the same token, the Christian is to look upon the elements as taking him back to the scenes of his redemption, as leading him to receive again the benefits of his Lord's passion, and as representing his response to that love which bore the Cross. Exodus xiii, 8 is a confession of 'that which the Lord did unto *me*', even though the participant of later Passover feasts had never personally set foot in Egypt, and had never known the wonder of the Red Sea miracle. The Corinthian believers – and the same is true of subsequent generations of Gentile Christians – had never been to the Palestine of Jesus' earthly ministry, never seen Him in His human form, in the days of His flesh (Hebrews v, 7), never sat at His table nor stood at His Cross. Yet by taking into their hands the things which He handled and hearing the words He spoke, and realizing that He is present by the Holy Spirit, we are *united* with Him in His atoning sacrifice and its potent benefits. All that His dying and rising accomplished for us is brought into the present tense; and each may say, 'He loved me and gave himself for me' (Galatians ii, 20). The crucified Lord is made apparent to our eyes in that sacrament which is especially reminiscent of His broken body and outpoured blood (Galatians iii, 1).

But the fellowship has a horizontal as well as a vertical reference. As we are knit with an unseen yet present Lord at His Table, so we are united with His people. This is the meaning of 1 Corinthians x, 17 (R.V. marg.): 'Seeing that there is one bread, we, who are many, are one body; for we all partake from the one loaf.' There is one loaf (Paul is saying) which is broken so that all who are present may have a share. But, he goes on, this common participation in a single loaf now joins you together as the spiritual counterpart of the one loaf. You are the body of Christ, the Church (Romans xii, 4, 5; Ephesians iv, 4–6; Colossians iii, 15). Therefore, there can be no justification for the divisions which plagued the Corinthian Church and disfigured its life even at the Table (1 Corinthians v, 6–8; xi, 17–22).

In the passage in 1 Corinthians x, 14–22, Paul is relating the teaching of the Supper to some pressing needs of his readers. The most obvious is the glaring disunity of the Church (1

Corinthians i, 10 ff.; iii, 3; iv, 6, 7; vi, 1 ff., etc.). This need is met as he points out how fellowship at a common table, and eating from a single loaf, are both meaningless practices except the Church comes to realize that this unity should become evident most clearly in these ways. In the same context, he addresses himself to another crying need of the Church; and this required some plain speaking about idolatry. The local background may be sketched in.*

The custom of taking a meal in a shrine dedicated to a cult deity, or of receiving wine which had been formally offered as a libation to a cult god, was a very popular one in the ancient Greco-Roman world. An Oxyrhynchus papyrus dated in the second century A.D. may be cited as a striking parallel to such an invitation as we have recorded in 1 Corinthians x, 27; 'If any of them that believe not bid you to a feast, and ye be disposed to go . . . .':

'Chaeremon invites you to dinner at the table of our lord Serapis (the cult god) in the Serapeum tomorrow the 15th at nine o'clock.'

Such an invitation to a meal,† whether in the temple or in a private house, would be commonplace in the social life of the city of Corinth.‡ For converted men – and perhaps, at times more acutely, for converted women – there was a problem posed by this custom. Should a Christian join in these feasts (many of them, the Corinthian Church told Paul, were harmless – they were on a par with the lunch engagements of the modern business-man), or may a Christian housewife buy in the market meat which had been left over from the sacrifice? This matter of daily shopping in Corinth is explicitly touched upon in 1 Corinthians x, 25 (the A.V. translation 'shambles' means 'meat-market'). Much of the meat which had been formally dedicated to the god in the temple would be sold by the temple officials to the meat dealers and would find its way to the market where it was exposed for sale. As sacrificial animals had to be free from blemish, it might well be the best meat in the market. But was the Christian housewife at liberty to purchase it?

The Apostle's answer to these practical problems is com-

* See N.B.D., art. 'Idols, Meat offered to,' p. 554 f. for more details of this background.

† Josephus records a similar invitation to a meal of Anubis in the Temple of Isis (*Ant.* xviii, 3, 4).

‡ The situation confronting the early Christians at Corinth is well set forth by Godet (quoted in J. Héring, *First Corinthians*, pp. 66 f.).

plex (1 Corinthians viii, 1–13; x, 18–33), but at least one ruling thought stands out in his consideration of these matters. This is that hands which have received the Communion bread should not be soiled with pagan rites which involve a compromise of Christian belief; and that lips which have tasted the wine are sealed against 'the cup of demons' (1 Corinthians x, 21). Fellowship at the Table is a pledge of loyalty and dedication to the Lord, whose table it is. The communicant is a committed person.

At an earlier stage in his dealing with the Corinthians' problems, Paul had faced another pastoral issue. What was he to do with a company of Christians who knowingly tolerated a notoriously immoral man in their Church? And actually were proud of that fact? 1 Corinthians v, 1 ff. describes the situation. St. Paul places his finger on the trouble by reminding them that they have forgotten the ritual of the Passover and the call to holiness which greets them at the Table of the Christian feast (1 Corinthians v, 7, 8). At the Paschal season every Jewish home is cleansed of all traces of leaven (following Exodus xii, 15; xiii, 7), and a solemn ritual is conducted as every nook arJ cranny of the home is searched and pronounced 'clean'.* This fact, Paul states, is true of the Christian. His 'old life' (Romans vi, 6; Ephesians iv, 22) is to be put away (2 Corinthians v, 17).† His new life is likened to an unleavened lump which is freed from all taint of leaven, a symbol here of evil, for he is reminded, as often as he keeps the festival of redemption (1 Corinthians v, 8), that Christ the Paschal Lamb calls him to a life which is pure and holy.‡ The

---

* The tractate *Pesachim i–ii* in the Mishnah (Danby's translation, pp. 136–39) speaks of the thorough search to be made in Jewish households immediately prior to Passover; and after the removing of all leaven and the scouring of utensils, the following declaration is to be made:

'May all leaven in my possession, whether I have seen it or not, or whether I have removed it or not, be annulled and considered as dust of the earth.'

† Romans vi is treated as a Christianized version of the Passover-Exodus experience of the proselyte who comes over into the Jewish faith by W. L. Knox, *St. Paul and the Church of the Gentiles* (Cambridge 1939), p. 87 ff. For the early Christian significance of the deliverance from Egypt, see C. H. Dodd, *According to the Scriptures* (London, 1952), p. 103. This has bearing on the Apostle's meaning in 1 Corinthians x, 1 ff.

‡ The imagery of unleavened bread = the new life in Christ is well brought out by J. Jeremias, *The Eucharistic Words of Jesus* (Oxford, E.T. 1955), p. 35.

anchoring of the Lord's Supper in a Passover setting could hardly be more evident.

(ii) The tradition which Paul received contained the words: 'This do ye . . . in remembrance of me' (1 Corinthians xi, 24, 25). His account goes on to interpret this: 'you proclaim the Lord's death until he comes' (verse 26). Both sentences are of consequence for our understanding of the ordinance; and both are to be seen on a Passover backcloth.

We have touched upon the meaning of 'remembrance', which contained for the Hebrew mind a dynamic aspect and was not simply a mental exercise. The case of the widow of Zarephath (1 Kings xvii, 18) is a good illustration of this dynamic quality. She accuses Elijah of 'recalling' her sin from the past; and the potency of this 'remembering' is seen in the death of her son. To recall, in Biblical thought, means to transport an action which is buried in the past in such a way that its original potency and vitality are not lost, but are carried over into the present. 'In remembrance of me', then, is no bare historical reflection upon the Cross, but a recalling of the crucified and living Christ in such a way that He is personally present in all the fulness and reality of His saving power, and is appropriated by the believers' faith.* The question now presses, how is this done?

The Apostolic answer lies in the words: 'ye proclaim the Lord's death' (R.V.). The A.V. translation which gives 'ye do shew' should be dropped, for it suggests that the Lord's Supper is a Passion play like the Mass, which it is not. The verb (*katangellein*) is the same as in 1 Corinthians ii, 1 where it is

---

* 'Remembrance was not for him (*sc.* Paul as an Israelite) mental recollection, an evocative thought. Remembrance was for him the restoration of a past situation which has for the moment disappeared. To remember is to make present and actual . . . It is possible for the past to become reactive'. So comments F. J. Leenhardt, 'This is My Body', in *Essays on the Lord's Supper* (by O. Cullmann and F. J. Leenhardt, London, E.T. 1958), p. 61 f.

When N. Clark expounds the term 'remembrance' (Gr. *anamnesis*) as 'the bringing of Christ crucified out of the past into the present, for the recalling of His sacrifice before God', he is in line with this thought, but his last two words (possibly derived from G. Dix, in *The Parish Communion*: ed. A. G. Hebert, London, 1937, p. 121) go beyond the evidence. See his *An Approach to the Theology of the Sacraments* (London, 1956), p. 62.

The 'remembrance' is with view to *our* appropriating Him by faith. For the Biblical sense of the term, see Douglas Jones' discussion in *Journal of Theological Studies*, n.s. vi, 1955, p. 183; and A. M. Stibbs *Sacrament, Sacrifice and Eucharist* (London, 1961), pp. 44 f.

rendered 'declare'; and indeed the verb is a usual one for the proclaiming of an event, the announcement of the Gospel. It is the death that is preached at the Table, not the dying of Jesus that is re-enacted.* And this emphasis has obvious links with the Passover Liturgy.

In that Liturgy, the tale of deliverance is to be retold; and as it is recounted, each individual Israelite relives the experience and makes his nation's history and destiny his very own.† At the Table, the story of the greater redemption is reported as often as we eat the bread and drink the cup.‡ The Cross ceases to be a judicial murder which occurred, e.g., on April the third, in the year 33 under the procuratorship of Pontius Pilate; it steps out of the frame of past history, and becomes present reality and personal fact. It confronts us as we sit at the Table with all that the death of the Son of God meant *then* and means *now*. Provided we insist on the importance of a living communion by faith, we may agree (in the light of the strong realism of 1 Corinthians x, 16) with Hauck's interpretation: 'Bread and wine are for Paul bearers of the presence of Christ'§ Later discussions of the nature of the Eucharistic presence are irrelevant in this context; and we should be content to state the simple fact without explanation, adding only that the Christ who is thus known at the Supper is the crucified and risen One. Any doctrine of His presence in the sacrament must be consonant with the total

* Markus Barth, quoted in Higgins, *The Lord's Supper in the New Testament*, p. 35.

† This notion of the (mystical) identification of the individual with the nation at the Passover as providing a most valuable clue to the Lord's Supper 'remembrance' has been worked out with great thoroughness by F. J. Leenhardt in his *Le Sacrement de la Sainte Cène* (Neuchâtel-Paris, 1948). The key-sentence is 'Every one of those who shared in the Paschal meal confessed that he had personally been the object of the redemption from Egypt' (op. cit. ,p. 38). See too W. D. Davies, *Paul and Rabbinic Judaism*, pp. 108 f., 252.

‡ G. Yetter (in *Z.N.T.W.*, 1913, p. 215) is able to write: 'The Lord's Supper is a sermon on the Cross,and an announcement of the death of Christ, an instruction which tells Christians that they are members of that new world created by His death.' But this view does not exclude the possibility that there was an explanatory verbal sermon (corresponding to the Passover *Haggadah*, or narration of the Exodus story) which accompanied the Supper. The Pauline verb, 'declare' could well be the equivalent of this Jewish term. C. H. Dodd comments: 'Some form of Passion-narrative accompanied the preaching of the Gospel and the celebration of the Sacrament' (*History and the Gospel*, London, 1938, p. 83). But the evidence for this is indirect: cf. Acts xx, 7 ff.

§ F. Hauck, art. in Kittel's *Wörterbuch*, III, p. 806.

Gospel emphasis on the spiritual union between the believer and his Lord in the fellowship of His body, the Church.*

(iii) 'Until he comes' (1 Corinthians xi, 26) unmistakably points to the future. The Gospel ordinance belongs to the Church age which will run its course until the inbreaking of the final Kingdom. Then the joy of a more direct fellowship with the living Lord will be known; and this is described under the figure of a banquet (Matthew xxvi, 29 and parallels; Revelation xix, 7–9, *etc.*). The Table bids the Church look to that day when the Kingdom will be fully consummated; and our invocation of *Marana tha* (Our Lord, come!) as a prayer for the End and the establishment of the Kingdom came naturally to find a place in the Communion services of the early Church.† The double thought of the Lord's presence at the Table and at the End of the Age runs through this primitive watchword.

Past, present and future are thus gathered up in one sacred and joyful festival of the Lord's Table in the Apostolic prac-

---

* In the section of 1 Corinthians xi, 27–32 we read of a situation at Corinth far different from the Pauline ideal. The key-word is 'unworthily' (verse 27). At the Church's common meal there was an absence of the spirit of considerateness and brotherhood, coupled with a tendency to excess and revelry. Some serious consequences followed his neglect of the deep seriousness of the occasion at the Lord's Table. The Corinthians were guilty of the body and blood of the Lord (verse 27); they ate and drank to their own judgement (verse 29); many of them had become ill and weak, and some had died (verse 30); and this judgement is taken by Paul to be a chastening by the Lord that a more fearful 'condemnation with the world' might be avoided (verse 32).

Various lines of interpretation have been offered. For instance, some think that the Corinthians had recklessly used the magically-charged sacramental elements of bread and wine. This is hardly correct. Or, it may be that the Lord's body in the context is the Church; and the gravamen of Paul's word (in verse 29) is that the careless people at Corinth have failed to discern the true nature of the Church as the body of Christ.

It may be suggested that the Exodus is still in Paul's mind. The judgement-power of the sacrament is then parallel with the judgements which overtook Pharaoh and the Egyptians. The Passover had a double effect; for the Jew in his house and joined to the people of God, it was a means of salvation; for the Egyptian outside and joined to his idols (Exodus xii, 12; Ezekiel xx, 8), it was a token of impending doom. So the unworthy behaviour of the Corinthians at the Christian Passover and the presence of many sins (idolatry; immorality; debauchery) were disruptive of the body of Christ, and were a standing denial of the Church's claim to be the new Israel, 'without leaven' (i.e. pure from the defilement of the outside world which in Paul's thought lies under the apocalyptic judgement of God, verse 32).

† See *Didache* x, 6.

tice and teaching. 'Indeed, in this Sacrament the whole of what our religion means is expressed'*; for one Lord Jesus Christ, incarnate, atoning and triumphant, is the sum and substance of it all.

* C. H. Dodd, in *Christian Worship* (ed N. Micklem: Oxford, 1936), p. 82.

12

Later Developments of Christian Worship

At the conclusion of our studies, we may seek to gather up the materials provided in the New Testament Scriptures into some pattern, to notice the main characteristic principles which underlie worship in the New Testament Church and to indicate the way in which future developments were tending.

The Church which meets us in the pages of the New Testament is a worshipping community of believing men and women. This is clear from the descriptions in the Acts of the Apostles (i, 14; ii, 42, 46; iv, 31; v, 12, 42; xiii, 1–3; xx, 7–12), and from the statements of Paul in his Letters (notably 1 Corinthians x–xiv). From these sources and the other Biblical material on which we have drawn in the preceding chapters, we learn that there were a number of distinctive features of early Christian public worship.

I. *Features of Early Christian Worship*

(i) There can be no doubt that the hall-mark which stamped the assembling together of Christians (Hebrews x, 25) as something for which no other religion can provide a parallel, was *the presence of the living Lord in the midst of His own* (Matthew xviii, 20; xxviii, 20). The promised word, 'There am I in the midst of them' was fulfilled as often as His people assembled in His name. He who was bodily absent (Mark xiv, 7) drew near in a special way as they met. All the component parts of divine service were calculated to lead the worshippers to an awareness of His presence.*

Confessions of faith proclaimed His lordship (Philippians ii, 11; Romans x, 9; 1 Corinthians xii, 3). The hymns and odes

---

* Compare G. Delling, *Worship in the New Testament* (London, E.T. 1962), p. 119.

praised both His person as the God-become-Man and His saving work by His death and resurrection (Philippians ii, 6–11; Colossians 1, 15–20; 1 Timothy iii, 16*). Prayer was offered in His name (John xv, 16; Ephesians v, 20; Hebrews xiii, 15). His word was declared (Colossians iii, 16) and His will sought (Ephesians iv, 20, 21). His invisible presence knit together Christian hearts (1 John i, 3), the outward sign for which fellowship was the common meal (1 Corinthians x, 17). In His name converts were baptized (Acts ii, 38) and admitted to the ranks of the Church (Romans xv, 7). At the Communion Table it was His Supper (1 Corinthians xi, 20) which was recalled and perpetuated; His death (1 Corinthians xi, 26) proclaimed and His body discerned (1 Corinthians xi, 29); and His future coming in glory awaited (1 Corinthians xi, 26).

Nothing is more characteristic of early Christian assemblies than the devotional exclamation *Marana tha* (1 Corinthians xvi, 22). This ejaculation may mean either, 'The Lord has come' (is coming), or (on the division of the letters as above) 'Our Lord, come!'† It looks backward to all that the coming of Christ into the world has meant, and is an acknowledgement of praise. It looks forward to His appearing, and is a cry of expectation. It has also a present significance, as it bids the assembled Church recognize that the Lord is in the midst and has come to greet His people.‡ The Christ-centred nature of Christian worship is one of the most clearly attested facts of the New Testament literature.

(ii) Yet all these devotional exercises were not the product of human endeavour and exertion alone. No amount of reflection and energy could have conjured up the presence of Christ if the assembling of Christians had not been directed by the Holy Spirit. Therefore, a second feature must be noted. New Testament worship *stands within 'the magnetic field of the Holy Spirit'* (in the expressive phrase of Professor van

* The work of Christ is set forth in early Christian hymns in terms of His cosmic redemption and victory over all spirit-forces in the universe. See *Vox Evangelica ii* (London, 1963), pp. 25 ff. and for this meaning of Christ's mission in Philippians ii, 6–11 the present writer's *Carmen Christi: Philippians ii, 5–11 in Recent Interpretation and in the setting of early Christian Worship* (Society for New Testament Study Monograph series, No. 3: Cambridge, 1966).

† For the meanings see O. Cullmann, *Christology of the New Testament* (London, E.T., 1959), p. 209.

‡ O. Cullmann, *Early Christian Worship* (London, E.T. 1953), p. 14 has noted the association of *Maranatha* with a meal, whichever interpretation be adopted.

Unnik*). Amid the diversity of forms and practices the presence and power of the Spirit of God are the decisive factors. He leads men to a confession of Jesus as Lord (1 Corinthians xii, 3); at the same time He checks any tendency to erroneous worship which seeks to offer to God what is unacceptable to Him. Examples of the later restraint are in 1 Corinthians xii, 3; xiv, 32 f.

The pervasive influence of the Spirit in Christian worship in the New Testament is worth observing. He inspires prayer (Romans viii, 26, 27; 1 Corinthians xiv, 15; Ephesians vi, 18; Jude 20); and opens the believer's mind and heart and voice in vocal praise (1 Corinthians xiv, 2, 15; Ephesians v, 19). It is by His ministry that we have access to the Father through the mediation of the Son (Ephesians ii, 18; Romans v, 2, 5; viii, 34; Hebrews vii, 25; 1 John ii, 1 f.) and are led into the deep truths of God's word (1 Corinthians ii, 10–16; John xvi, 13 ff.), as He imparts to some fellow-believer who has the gift of teaching (Romans xii, 7; Ephesians iv, 11 ff.) the word of wisdom and knowledge (1 Corinthians xii, 8). Moreover, He is the Spirit of prophecy (i.e. in this context, convincing speech, designed to expound the sacred truth of God to men for their benefit. 1 Corinthians xiv, 3 gives this sense. See 1 Corinthians ii, 4; 1 Thessalonians i, 5; Acts xvii, 24–28 for illustration). And His effectual presence in a Church service when prophecy is made leads the unbeliever or outsider to fall down under conviction and yield to God (1 Corinthians xiv, 25; John xvi, 8 ff.)

St. Paul sums up the importance of the Holy Spirit in public worship when he says simply: 'We worship by the Spirit of God' (Philippians iii, 3, R.V.; compare John iv, 24).

(iii) A third feature of worship in the Pauline Churches is *the concern for upbuilding*. If we take the Corinthian Church as a norm, we may notice three components of Christian worship in that community.

There was (a) *the charismatic element*. By this term we mean the offering of enthusiastic praise and prayer under the direct afflatus of the Spirit, whether in intelligible or ecstatic language (i.e. *glossolalia*, or the gift of 'tongues', referred to in 1 Corinthians xiv, 2, 6 ff.). While he does not censure this latter form of worship, Paul insists that there must be an

---

* W. C. van Unnik, art. '*Dominus Vobiscum:* The Background of a Liturgical Formula', *New Testament Essays in Memory of T. W. Manson* (ed. A. J. B. Higgins, Manchester, 1959), p. 294.

accompanying interpretation (xiv, 5, 13, 28) so that the Church may benefit and be edified (verse 5). Otherwise, 'speaking in tongues' is a waste of time (verses 6, 9) – or worse (verse 23)!

Then (b) there is *the didactic side*. This covers all ministry in intelligible speech which aims at clarifying the will of God, whether by teaching (1 Corinthians xii, 8), instructing (1 Corinthians xiv, 26), prophesying (i.e. what we would call preaching, 1 Corinthians xi, 4, 5; xiv, 3) and discerning the truth (1 Corinthians xiv, 29; cf.; 1 Thessalonians v, 21; 1 John iv, 1). Added to this is the offering of prayer (1 Corinthians xi, 4, 5; xiv, 15). In all phases of this type of worship, the same rubric applies: 'Let all things be done for edification' (1 Corinthians xiv, 26).

The third element (c) is *eucharistic*, which is the offering of a *Jubilate* of thanksgiving (as the name implies), whether by prayer (1 Corinthians xiv, 16); hymns and canticles (Ephesians v, 19–20; Colossians iii, 16, 17. These two texts fill out the bare mention in 1 Corinthians xiv, 26; cf. earlier in that chapter verse 15); or the distinctive Christian ordinance of the Lord's Supper (1 Corinthians xi, 18 ff.). Here again the Apostolic insistence is that all shall be for the Church's good and upbuilding – an ideal which the Corinthians had failed to reach because of selfishness (xi, 20–22) and insensitive carelessness at the Table with its solemn associations (xi, 27–30). Written large over all Paul's recommendation and directives for public worship at Corinth are the words: 'Strive for the upbuilding of the Church' (xiv, 12).

We have surveyed the chief constituents of early Christian public and corporate worship in its many facets and forms. Hans Lietzmann's dictum seems well-founded. 'The heart of the Christian life is to be found in the act of public worship.'* To justify this concurrence let us recall the three terms which sum up Christian acts of public devotion. In the charismatic ministry of the Holy Spirit He opened the lips of the first believers to pray and to praise, with the theme of God's saving action in Jesus Christ the *leitmotiv* of this exultation. The second word – the didactic aspect – denotes the instructional side of public assembly, as Christians gathered in order to be taught the things of God by those whom God raised up as Apostles, prophets and teachers in the Churches, or else believers met to search the Scriptures and to hear the writings of

* H. Lietzmann, *The Founding of the Church Universal* (London, E.T. 1950), p. 124.

the Apostles read to them. The term 'eucharistic' relates to the note of thankfulness and joy which must have sounded in the early Christian convocations. The thanksgiving was expressed either by vocal utterances (as in hymns or in prayer) or the giving of money for the Lord's service, or (in ways which He appointed) the observance of sacred and solemn 'portrayals' which set forth the Gospel message in acted symbolism – the ordinance of Baptism, speaking of death and resurrection; the ordinance of the holy Supper, proclaiming the Lord's death until He shall come, and testifying to His living presence in the midst of His people who break bread 'in remembrance of' Him. Both sacraments were calculated to call forth a divine *sursum corda* – up with your heart! – as the Church's grateful acknowledgement of and response to God for His mercy in Christ, although it is the latter service which came quickly to be known as 'the Thanksgiving' (the Eucharist).

Although these three components make up the whole of early Christian worship, there is, of course, no place in the New Testament which clearly states that the Church had any set order of service, and very little information is supplied to us about the outward forms which were in use. The use of musical instruments is a case in point. While there are allusions made to certain instruments (for example, the harp or lyre, the pipe, the cymbal, the trumpet – and possibly the 'noisy gong' of 1 Corinthians xiii, 1*), there is no certainty that any of these were actually used. The balance of probability is against such a use.†

The New Testament writers are far more concerned with the principles of worship and with the spirit which motivates the offering of praise to God. Two features stand out.

First, there is repeated emphasis upon the 'together-ness' of believers, which runs like a thread through the Acts of the Apostles (i, 14; ii, 46; iv, 24; v, 12; viii, 6; xv, 25) and is found in the Epistles (Romans xv, 6; 1 Corinthians v, 4; xi, 20; xiv, 23). The phrases used in the last references imply both physical proximity – together in one place – and a oneness of heart and mind.

The second important feature arises naturally from this insistence upon the unity of the Spirit. The dominating concern

* W. S. Smith, *Musical Aspects of the New Testament* (Amsterdam, 1962), pp. 43 ff. and passim has exhaustively studied the references in 1 Corinthians xiii; xiv and Revelation v, 8; xiv, 2; xv, 2; xviii, 22, etc.
† So C. F. D. Moule, *Worship in the New Testament*, p. 65.

in public worship is to glorify God and to seek the welfare of the whole fellowship of the Church. The thought that the Church at worship is an accidental convergence in one place of a number of isolated individuals who practise, in hermetically sealed compartments, their own private devotional exercises, is foreign to the New Testament picture. The key-term which gives the lie to such a false picture is 'upbuilding' or 'edification', which as we have seen is to the forefront of the Apostles' mind in 1 Corinthians (see xii, 7; xiv, 3–5, 12, 17, 26). He is at pains to point out that the truly corporate aspect of worship is the important thing. It is not a case of the individual seeking his own ends. He must remember that he worships as an individual who is a member within the body of Christ. This rule puts a check upon selfishness and the gratification of personal tastes; it is equally a reminder that we all have a part to play. Professor E. Schweizer has recently shown that most of modern worship is defective at this point. 'It is completely foreign to the New Testament to split the Christian community into one speaker and a silent body of listeners,' he comments.*

Because there is no extant 'Church Order' within the pages of the New Testament canon, it may seem futile to speak about any development in the customs and practices of the New Testament Churches. But there are some pointers.

II. *Developments of Worship Within the New Testament Period*

There are three notable landmarks which show the way in which Christians emphasized one or other of the chief elements.†

(i) 1 Thessalonians v, 16–22 is a section to be studied carefully. We notice the way in which the short sentences are framed. In the original Greek, the verb in each sentence stands last. There is a predominance of words which begin with the Greek letter 'p', thus giving a rhythm. The order of the injunctions, 'Pray, give thanks' and 'Do not discourage

* E. Schweizer, art. 'Worship in the New Testament', *The Reformed and Presbyterian World*, xxiv, 5, 1957, p. 295. This essay is deserving of close attention, with its emphasis on the New Testament ideal of fellowship-in-worship.

† I am indebted to Professor James M. Robinson of Southern California School of Theology for some seminal thoughts which produced this section.

prophecy, but test the utterances' is particularly to be noted.

When the passage is set down in lines, it reads as though it contained the 'headings 'of a Church service. The note of glad adoration is struck at the opening: 'Rejoice always' (verse 16). Prayer and thanksgiving are coupled – a trait which comes into the Church from the synagogue assembly. Christians are coun- selled to give the Spirit full rein, especially as He opens the mouths of the prophets (verses 19, 20); but cautioned (verse 21) that they must test the spirits (cf. 1 John iv, 1). Above all, nothing unseemly must enter the assembly (verse 22), but all should be done 'decently and in order' (1 Corinthians xiv, 40). And the closing part of this 'Church order' – if this description is correct – contains a comprehensive prayer for the entire fellowship (verse 23), expressed in the confidence that God will hear and bless (verse 24).

(ii) The singular thing is that, when we turn to 1 Corinthians xiv, a similar series of Apostolic counsels on the subject of public worship meets us. The custom of praise and 'hymning' is mentioned (verses 14, 15), and both practices are inspired by the Spirit (as we are to infer from 1 Thessalonians v, 19). Prayer and thanksgiving are found in that order (verses 13– 18) and prophecy and the testing of utterances (verses 27 ff.) are also linked, as in the Letter to the Thessalonians. It is true that the injunction 'Quench not the Spirit' is not alluded to, but this omission may be explained by the fact at Corinth there was not the danger that the Spirit's more spectacular gifts in worship were being neglected – quite the reverse! But there is another link between the two 'Church orders' (again using the later term). It may well be that 1 Corinthians xiv, 34–36, 40 (the command for women to keep silence in the worship) has to do with the same situation as is envisaged in 1 Thessalonians v, 21, namely, the need to test the pro- phecies, especially if the women members of the Church at Corinth were those who, like the daughters of Philip (Acts xxi, 9), possessed the prophetic gift. It may be, then, that (in view of 1 Corinthians xiv, 32, 33) some women had abused the gift; and Paul warns against unseemly behaviour in an assembly where the public worship could quickly get out of hand (as in 1 Corinthians xi, 17 ff.) and notably where women were concerned (as in 1 Corinthians xi, 5–16). The same may have been true later at Ephesus in view of 1 Timothy ii, 8 ff.

(iii) The witness of Colossians iii, 16–18 may be brought in, for the same verb is used there (and in the parallel text, Ephesians v, 19 ff.) as in 1 Corinthians xiv, 34b. : wives are called to be submissive to their husbands. The noun 'submission' recurs in 1 Timothy ii, 11. It is worth noting that, in these later Epistles, the stress falls on 'teaching and exhortation' (Colossians iii, 16). Hymns are encouraged, and the need of Christians to be filled with the Spirit (Ephesians v, 18) in order that the songs which are sung will be acceptable worship as 'odes inspired by the Spirit' (Ephesians v, 19; Colossians iii, 16) is taught; but there is some limitation placed on this type of praise. Ecstatic speech – 'speaking in tongues' – is never hinted at. What is permitted at Thessalonica (with the caution to test the spirits), and given a tolerated status at Corinth, is ignored completely in the later Letters.

The conclusion seems inescapable that the Church is moving out of a situation in which the pattern of worship is pliant and free, under the direct afflatus of the Holy Spirit and with each believer making a contribution as seems good to him (with all the attendant perils which surround such a liberty) into an area of experience that comes with organization and development, and where the worship (though no less Spirit-inspired and real) will be offered according to recognized 'canons'.

Some of these rubrics are found in Colossians iii, 16, which emphasizes the importance of the written Word, the ministry of instruction, and a more varied pattern of hymnic praise (perhaps including the use of the Old Testament Psalter) than at Corinth (1 Corinthians xiv, 15; but compare verse 26). Certain features remain, and are the permanent inheritance of the Church in every age. These are: thanksgiving (Colossians iii, 15–17), the vocal expression of gratitude to God (Colossians iii, 16) and mutual instruction and edification (Ephesians v, 19; cf. Romans xv, 14, R.S.V. and Colossians iii, 16). And with these aspects of Christian worship in its outword form, the inner meaning should be remembered. This is clearly stated in Romans xii, 1: 'I appeal to you . . . to present your bodies as a living sacrifice, holy and acceptable to God, which is your spiritual worship' (R.S.V.). The addition of the adjective 'spiritual' seems to be in contrast with Romans ix, 4 where Israel's cultic system is described as 'the worship'. Christian worship is essentially inward and spiritual, whatever outward forms and ceremonies may or may not be used.

This emphasis is found at its most insistent in a New Testament document which sets forth the message of the Gospel in

terms of man's relationship to God as a spiritual worshipper –
the Letter to the Hebrews. Such a relationship is made possible
by the one Sacrifice which ends all sacrifices (Hebrews x,
12 ff.). But one cultic office does remain: 'the sacrifice of
praise continually to God, that is, the fruit of lips that acknowledge His name' (Hebrews xiii, 15 f.).

The Apocalypse of John is full of echoes of heavenly worship which sound the note of adoring praise to God as
Creator (iv, 8–11) and Redeemer (v, 9–14). The Church on
earth shares in this exultant acknowledgement in the exercise
of its priestly ministry (i. 6).

III. *Developments of Christian Worship in the Second
Century*
The intensely interesting topic of the evolution of Christian
worship in the period following the New Testament era would
require another book, if justice were to be done to it. A closing
section of a book which is exclusively concerned with the
Biblical data can only indicate some of the main trends.*

(i) *The Standardizing of Worship*
We have already noticed that there is no apparent 'Church
Order' in the New Testament. In the enigmatic document
known as the *Didache* whose date may be placed anywhere in
the century A.D. 50–150 – but most probably around the year
100 – the pattern of such an order of service at the Communion
(integrated with a common meal, called the *Agape* or love-
feast) emerges. Set prayers are given and are intended to be
used at the Table. But there is sufficient liberty for a rubric to
be added: 'But let the prophets give thanks as much as they
desire,' i.e. the prophets are unfettered by the prescribed
prayers.† But the order of prophets is on the way out, and in
a letter written by Clement of Rome to Corinth (about A.D. 96)
we hear the sounds of a conflict and tension between an
itinerant ministry (the prophets) and a regular, local ministry,
appointed by the Church and claiming some prescriptive right
to conduct Church services without interference. And the

* The historical developments are set out in J. H. Srawley *The Early
History of the Liturgy* (Cambridge, 1947) and W. D. Maxwell, *An
Outline of Christian Worship* (Oxford, 1936).
† *Didache* x, 7.

future lies with the later, as Clement makes clear. The same document contains a lengthy prayer of general intercessions which borrows a number of expressions from the Old Testament – a feature which became a common liturgical practice.

Within the next half century the pattern of worship must have hardened (though we have no documentary evidence from Christian sources of the period A.D. 100–150). At least by the time of Justin (about A.D. 150), a definite order of Scripture readings, sermons by the leader, common prayers under some direction, the offering of bread and wine to 'the president' who in turn leads the people in thanksgiving for creation and redemption, the distribution of the elements by the deacons to the people, and the collection for the needy, is well known and has become standardized. The day of the spontaneously offered worship in which all the members of the congregation share at will (as in 1 Corinthians xiv) is over; and we are approaching the era of service-books and liturgies.

(ii) *The Attitude to the Lord's Supper*

The literature of the second century is full of a vocabulary which is never found in the New Testament. The *Didache* calls the Lord's table a 'sacrifice', regarding this term as appropriate in view of Malachi i, 11, 14.* This attribution set a precedent which led eventually to the full-blown doctrine of the Eucharistic sacrifice in the later Fathers of the Church.† Ignatius lays it down, shortly after the turn of the century, that the Eucharist is not to be celebrated apart from the bishop; and the Church is, in his view, 'a place of sacrifice'.‡ Even more pronounced are the teachings of Justin who gives expression to the notion that the bread and the cup are transmuted by a formula of consecration and have power to infuse the divine life into the souls and bodies of the faithful.§ The real presence tends, from this point of the development onwards, to be located not in a spiritual reception of Christ by faith, but in the elements themselves.

Yet the picture is not simply one of continual deterioration and decline from Apostolic standards. The group of Christians

---

* *Didache* xiv, 1–3. This Old Testament quotation was ascribed evidently to Christ.
† See *Eucharistic Sacrifice* (ed. J. I. Packer. London, 1962) pp. 71 ff.
‡ Ignatius, *Smyrnaeans* viii; *Magnesians* vii, 2; *Philad.* iv.
§ Justin, *First Apology* lxvi.

in Bithynia in A.D. 112 who met simply to sing a hymn to
Christ as God and to share a common meal on a set day, re-
nouncing evil practices as the Lord's people,* are the spiritual
kin of first century believers, and offer an attractive picture
and paradigm to us today.

* See the discussion of this text from Pliny, *Ep.* x, 96 (in Betty Radice's
translation of Penguin Classic, 1963, p. 294) by the present writer, art.
'A Footnote to Pliny's Account of Christian Worship', *Vox Evangelica*
iii (London, 1964), pp. 51–57.

Index

A. SUBJECTS

B. PRINCIPAL SCRIPTURAL PASSAGES CONSIDERED

C. MODERN AUTHORS